Prairie Twins

Alberta and Saskatchewan Photographic Memories
1905 ~ 2005

Faye Reineberg Holt

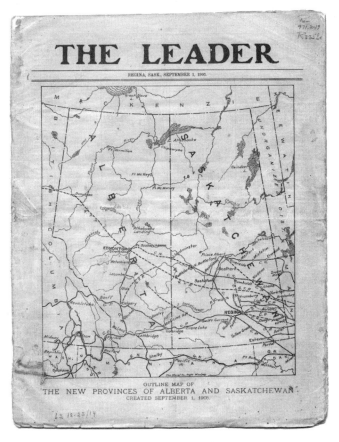

THE LEADER

REGINA, SASK., SEPTEMBER 1, 1905.

OUTLINE MAP OF
THE NEW PROVINCES OF ALBERTA AND SASKATCHEWAN
CREATED SEPTEMBER 1, 1905.

The Leader map for Inauguration of Provinces, 1905.
Glenbow Library, Calgary Canada, Pam 971.249 R335 LE#

DETSELIG
ENTERPRISES LTD.

Prairie Twins: Alberta and Saskatchewan Photographic Memories, 1905-2005
© 2004 Faye Reineberg Holt

Library and Archives Canada Cataloguing in Publication

Reineberg Holt, Faye
  Prairie twins : Alberta and Saskatchewan photographic memories, 1905-2005/
Faye Reineberg Holt

Includes bibliographical references and index.

ISBN 1-55059-267-X

  1. Alberta–History–Pictorial works. 2. Saskatchewan–History–Pictorial works.
3. Alberta–Pictorial works. 4. Saskatchewan–Pictorial works. I. Title.

FC3237.R47 2004   971.23'0022'2   C2004-905773-1

Detselig Enterprises Ltd.
210, 1220 Kensington Road NW
Calgary, Alberta T2N 3P5
Phone: (403) 283-0900
Fax: (403) 283-6947
Email: temeron@telusplanet.net
www.temerondetselig.com

We acknowledge the support of the Government of Canada through the Book Publishing Industry Development Program (BPIDP) for our publishing program.

We also acknowledge the support of the Alberta Foundation for the Arts for our publishing program.

COMMITTED TO THE DEVELOPMENT OF CULTURE AND THE ARTS

ISBN 1-55059-267-X
SAN 113-0234
Printed in Canada

Front photo: Hanna Museum, PH-44
Back photo, top: Saskatoon Public Library, LH 4064
Back photo, bottom: Glenbow Archives, Calgary, Canada, NC 29 77

Cover design: Alvin Choong

Dedication

To Great Friends

Thank you for just being there, for your encouragement, and for sharing your perceptions, knowledge, and stories.

Special Thanks

To my publisher Ted Giles, my editor Kim Robertson, the staff of Glenbow Archives and Library for outstanding service, the staff of the many other archives, and those who contributed photos.

Cable ferry. *Brooks Museum*

In early Edmonton, participants in the Canadian Press Club picnic of about 1919 enjoyed a trip on the river as part of their outing. *Glenbow Archives, Calgary, Canada, NC 6-519*

Table of Contents

Photo: Glenbow Archives, Calgary, Canada, PA-1599-3-15

ROY ROGERS LIBERTY HORSES

Trainer—Glenn Randall

Famous people and animals, such as Roy Rogers and Trigger, were invited to events. Shown here in 1954, Roy Rogers Liberty Horses provided a memorable performance at the Edmonton Exhibition. *City of Edmonton Archives, EA 45-195*

Television and movies impacted the provinces bringing entertainment and employment. *Saskatchewan Archives Board, Rusty MacDonald Photo, S-RM-A-1682*

Twins

One Landscape, Two Provinces

Alberta and Saskatchewan are twins with the same day, September 1, 1905, for a birthday. By no means identical, they are more alike than different. Geographically, they are the only provinces in Canada that do not have a saltwater coast. Both have desert-like prairie, vast grasslands, treed and vibrant parkland, and boreal forests, plus subarctic areas in their far north.

In areas on the same latitude, the twins share weather patterns. With the exception of the Chinook belt, they experience much the same weather in spring, summer, autumn, and winter. Both are sunshine provinces. With equally long days in summer, they can brag about hours of sunshine. Saskatchewan averages 2 540 hours per year, and Alberta has just as many sunny skies.

Building the provinces has been a shared history for Alberta and Saskatchewan. In 1908, together, settlers at Pense, Saskatchewan, built this barn. *Saskatchewan Archives Board, R-A 4313*

Their landscape is significantly different only where the narrow ridge on Alberta's western boundary blends into the Rockies of British Columbia. Then again, in Saskatchewan's far northeast, the more easterly twin shares a little of the Canadian Shield with its Manitoba neighbor. Although there are similarities with their sister prairie province, Manitoba, neither Alberta nor Saskatchewan has as many lakes or the influence of a great bay of water.

The wildlife recognized no boundaries and flourished, or became threatened or extinct in both provinces. Their First Nations recognized no boundary and had a shared history. Explorers, fur and whiskey traders, Mounties, and railroaders influenced the history in similar ways. They and aboriginal people travelled trails that long united the landscape and eventually took names such as the Carlton Trail and Boundary Commission Trail. White settlers arrived in the area of the North-West Territories that would become the two provinces at about the same time. There were similar ethnic back-

For its motto, Saskatchewan looked to its skies and became "The Land of the Living Skies," but that sky brought much the same weather on both sides of the Alberta-Saskatchewan border. This photo by renowned Saskatchewan photographer and former editor of the *Western Producer*, Thomas Melville-Ness, captures the moodiness of prairie skies. For many, the *Western Producer* was the voice of the prairie. *Saskatchewan Archives Board,S-MN-B 515.*

grounds among most of the newcomers.

In both provinces, the most northern boundary is the 60th parallel, and the most southerly boundary is the 49th parallel, while the 110th meridian divides them. Whether in the north, central, or south areas of the provinces, along the border between them, there is no discernable difference in landscape when viewed from the sky. For its motto, Alberta chose "Wild Rose Country," but the flora and fauna recognized no borders, and the wild flowers and animals are much the same in the two provinces.

In areas of the twin provinces, flat land extends to the horizon and beyond. Underground similarities exist too. Both have petroleum resources, but there is an Alberta Advantage. The Saskatchewan's advantage is potash since significant deposits have not been found in Alberta. *Faye Holt Photo*

Mighty Saskatchewan
& Other Waterways

In 1924, renowned Banff photographer Byron Harmon captured the majesty of the Saskatchewan Glacier. *Whyte Museum of the Canadian Rockies,V 263-NA 71-2227*

At their northern boundary, on the border between Alberta and Saskatchewan, the provinces share the waters of Lake Athabasca. As well, the twins are linked by the prairies' great river systems. The most important river links between them are the tributaries of the Saskatchewan.

The First Nations word *kisiskatchewan* meaning "the river that flows swiftly," referred to the mighty Saskatchewan River. Not only was that name bestowed on the river and its tributaries, the North and South Saskatchewan, it became the name of a glacier, an important historical fort, and a province. Century after century, melt water from Saskatchewan Glacier in the Columbia Icefield, winter run off, and rain have created and recreated the North Saskatchewan River.

Other waterways including the Battle, Red Deer, and Clearwater rivers meandered through both provinces, but the Saskatchewan River system joined the far west of Alberta and the far east of Saskatchewan. The most important early "highway" between the two

Construction of this boat took place at Athabasca, Alberta. Because lakes and rivers were the first highways, boat building was a significant industry, especially in northern areas of the provinces. At Edmonton, the Northern Boat Building Company was very active from the teens to the 1930s. The company shipped boats on railway flat bed cars as far as Fort Norman in the Northwest Territories. *Alice B. Donahue Library and Archives, Athabasca, AB, 940*

provinces, the waterway carried fur traders, missionaries, surveyors, settlers, and adventurers.

Many rivers influenced the growth of both Alberta and Saskatchewan, but the North Saskatchewan dramatically influenced settlement at Edmonton, Battleford, and Prince Albert. The South Saskatchewan River had an equivalent influence on the development of Calgary and Saskatoon. At the confluence of the two tributaries, the "Mighty Saskatchewan" itself created their link to Manitoba. Finally, those waters spilled into the Hudson's Bay, with all its historic ties to the fur trade.

Badlands and Monster Bones

Alberta and Saskatchewan mirrored each other in much of their pre-history, and both can brag about their badlands and dinosaurs. Over centuries, with little vegetation, the hills of shale and sandstone eroded. Named badlands by early explorers, the strange landscape revealed the geological layers of earth and a once tropical environment. This also exposed the bones of great dinosaurs and the area proved an excellent fossil hunting grounds.

By the mid 1870s, surveyors with the International Boundary Commission found many fossil remains on the prairies near what became the American border. The first dinosaur bone discovery in Saskatchewan was in 1874 at Killdeer Badlands, but early on, Alberta became the most significant dinosaur hunting grounds. By 1884, working with the Geographical Survey of Canada, Joseph Tyrrell discovered a skull for a dinosaur that became named Albertosaurus. By the early 1900s, already well known and acclaimed, C. H. Sternberg and his sons Levi and Charles M. began their hunt for fossils in western Canada on behalf of American museums. The first fossils they collected were sent to the States. Geological Survey of Canada offered contracts to C.M. and Levi, who continued the work for the Canadian government, and were later contracted by Canadian museums and universities. The work was often tedious and difficult. First there was finding the fossils. Then the treasures had to be carefully removed. They were weighed, photographed, boxed, and shipped to the USA or Ontario for further scholarly study.

Significant fossil-rich areas included the Belly River and Cypress Hills areas of Alberta and Saskatchewan. There, early relatives of modern rhinoceros, pigs, deer, and crocodiles formed part of the rich heritage. Bones of the Mosasaurus Condon were found

Left: Because of fossils, the Drumheller Valley became a UNESCO world heritage site. Today, the town of Drumheller uses a dino motif to promote tourism. Dinosaurs are everywhere—even coming out the wall of the IGA grocery store. *Walt Holt Photo*

Right: Discovering the massive jawbone of a dinosaur made the work rewarding. *Brooks Museum, P5-06*

near Saskatchewan Landing, but discoveries made at Steveville on the Red Deer River were most impressive. The Badlands of the Drumheller Valley proved to be one of the richest dinosaur hunting areas of the world. Important fossil remains of the Edmontosaurus, Tyrannosaurus rex, and Chasmosaurus were unearthed in Alberta.

Fossil hunting in Saskatchewan, came into its own and proved enormously successful in the 1990s. In 1991, near Eastend, Saskatchewan at the Frenchman River Valley, the bones of a Tyrannosaurus rex were found. From 1994

Unearthing fossils was painstaking and time-consuming work for Sternberg and his team member. *Brooks Museum, P5-05*

Above: Staff of Tyrrell Museum have made use of vividly painted backdrops, recreating scenes of a lush prairie environment inhabited by different types of dinosaurs. Sculptures reconstruct the skeletal remains indicating the animal's shape and hint of the science of palaentology. *Walt Holt photo.*

Right: Children remain fascinated by the story of dinosaurs in western Canada. Here, a life-like replica of the T-Rex at Tyrrell Museum, Drumheller, Alberta, dwarfs Jeremy of Edmonton. *Walt Holt photo.*

to 1995, experts excavated the entire skeleton of a T-rex, nicknamed Scotty. Since then, at the newly constructed T-Rex Discovery Centre, which is about the size of a skating rink, fossils are on display.

Preserving the
Majestic Landscape

The western boundary of Alberta is the only area where extreme geographical differences exist between the two provinces. For Saskatchewan and Alberta vacationers, a longtime favorite destination has been Banff and Lake Louise. However, countless national and international travellers have enjoyed summer and winter holidays in the Rockies. Photographer Byron Harmon captured an Alpine Club of Canada hike to the giant steps of Paradise Valley at Banff National Park in 1907. *Whyte Museum of the Canadian Rockies, V 263-N611-60*

Weather Wonderland

A fact of life in Canada, cold winter weather seldom surprises Alberta and Saskatchewan residents. More distressing is that either snow or hail can drift from the sky every month of the year. Freak snow storms might dump 40-65 centimetres (16- 26 inches) of snow in a 24 hour period. Willmar, Saskatchewan, received 40.6 centimetres (16 inches) of snow on a May day in 1923. Moosomin witnessed the same single-day accumulation in April, 1945. Locals in Cardston, Alberta, were shocked in 1950 when May brought 63.5 centimetres (25 inches) of snow in 24 hours. In 1960, High River, Alberta, had 46 centimetres (18 inches) on a single day. Qu'Appelle, Saskatchewan, recorded 62 centimetres (24 inches) in March, 1971. The heavy spring snowfalls generally melted quickly, but that could create another problem – flooding.

Countless communities situated on riverbanks in the two provinces suffered flood damage.

Heavy snowfalls, such as this near Fort Saskatchewan, Alberta, caused serious problems for travellers since clearing roads, railways, and runaways was time consuming, difficult work. *Milt Moyer Collection*

On March 24, 1943, when flood water hit Rosedale near Drumheller, Alberta, Mr. Preisic carried his wife to dry land. *Glenbow Archives, Calgary, Canada NA 4741-1*

The great Saskatchewan, and North and South Saskatchewan rivers have all flooded. So did smaller rivers, such as the Belly River [Old Man River] at Lethbridge, Alberta, where during the summer of 1902, the river flooded on three separate occasions.

In 1899, 1915, and 2004, Edmonton was hit by devastating floods. The flood in 1915 was caused by melt waters and heavy rain raising the river level. The river overflowed onto the flats and left 2 400 people homeless.

The flood on July 11, 2004, was also devastating to Edmontonians, but it was not caused by the river overflowing its banks. Instead, torrential rains combined with pounding hail. Just before 3:00 p.m., the brief storm pounded the city. With 15 centimetres (6 inches) of rain, as well as hail the size of golf balls, drains clogged and backed up.

Battered, the roof of West Edmonton Mall was damaged and leaked. More water gushed from the indoor ice arena. With public areas awash in as much as 46 centimetres (18 inches) of water, 20 000 people had to be evacuated.

The damage as a result of water backing up from blocked sewers seemed beyond belief. In low areas under bridges, rising water levels floated cars. One man returning from a canoe trip took the canoe from his car roof and rescued stranded drivers and their families.

Elsewhere, water backed up and flooded thousands of basements. Once damage was assessed, total insurance claims mounted to $60 million, but for thousands who had lost prized possessions and keepsakes stored in their basements, life would never be quite the same.

Cyclone Alley

Canada ranks second only to the USA in terms of tornado occurrences. Ontario and other provinces suffer serious tornados, but Alberta and Saskatchewan have ideal conditions for the big winds. Cyclones have occurred at many prairie locations, but tornado alley for Alberta runs from south of Calgary to just north of Edmonton. At risk in Saskatchewan is a similar corridor between Saskatoon and slightly south of Regina. In earlier times, with communication limited and

On July 8, 1927, this cyclone approached Vulcan, Alberta. Normally, the province averages 16 tornadoes of varying strength per year. In 1927, central Alberta was hit by 40 tornadoes. *Saskatoon Public Library PH 91-286-2*

populations sparse and far-flung, only large tornadoes were widely reported. But twister history in the twin provinces is a long one.

In Saskatchewan, settlers recorded a tornado in June, 1898. It wreaked havoc at Wolseley and caused the death of one person at Percy. At Eagle Creek, another touched down in July of 1904. One hit Delisle, Saskatchewan, in 1910.

The worst twister in the history of the two provinces descended on Regina. The last week in June, 1912, the heat was blistering. Day after day, Regina had endured 32° C (90°F) and above temperatures. Such weather burned young crops, but it couldn't put a kibosh on plans for July 1, Dominion Day, celebrations. As they approached, enthusiasts put up the usual "bunting" and decorations for the summer festivity. By midday on June 30, Regina was ready but staying cool was also a priority.

Some had gone boating or swimming in Lake Wascana to escape the heat. Others took refuge in their homes or places of business. For many, spending the evening outdoors was the only time they escaped the searing heat.

Around 4:00 p.m., clouds from the southeast and southwest approached, filling the sky. Then, the cyclone descended on the city. Glass shattered. Homes were torn apart. Other buildings crashed to the ground. The grain elevator was flattened. Debris filled the air. Clocks stopped. The consequences of the tornado were devastating. Rescue and medical workers were run off their feet. All had changed in those few seconds. In total, twenty-eight people died, and parts of the city had to be totally rebuilt.

Between 1890 and 1989, Regina experienced tornado incidents seventeen times, Saskatoon ten times, and Moose Jaw on six occasions.

Alberta had always suffered similar woes. A cyclone hit MacLaughlin about 1903. A school in Nanton was pulled off its foundations in about 1915. During one twister in 1918, three children died at Vermilion.

Edmonton has been in the path of tornadoes twelve times between 1890 and 1989. The worst tornado in Alberta hit Edmonton during the late afternoon on June 31, 1987. The twister created a swath over 37 kilometers (23 miles) long. Wind and hail, some as large as tennis balls, pounded East Edmonton's industrial area. Parts of the city were paralyzed when the winds brought down power lines. Buildings were flattened, and vehicles wrecked. Twenty-seven people died, only one fewer than in Regina's 1912 disaster.

In 2000, campers and locals at Pine Lake, Alberta, suffered the devastation of a tornado in the early evening of July 14. Over the years, Calgary has had three serious tornado warnings, Lethbridge has had two episodes, and Medicine Hat has faced possible disaster on four occasions. According to Environment Canada, the prairie provinces average forty-one tornadoes a year.

Collapsed buildings were part of the aftermath of the Regina Cyclone.
Saskatchewan Archives Board, R.J. Lindsay Photo R-B 3720

100 Years Later
Emblems & Symbols

Over the years, both Alberta and Saskatchewan legislatures enacted laws establishing official symbols, emblems, coat of arms, and flags for their provinces. In terms of the nature-based emblems, most of the animals, birds, trees, and grasses chosen by one province could just as easily represent the other. An exception is potash, the mineral for Saskatchewan, since the province produces 95 percent of the potash in Canada.

Alberta Symbols	Saskatchewan Symbols
Motto: Strong and free (*Fortis et liber*)	**Motto**: From many people many strengths (*Multis e gentibus vires*)
Bird: Great horned owl	**General symbol**: Sheaf of wheat
Cloth: Alberta tartan	**Bird**: Sharp-tailed grouse
Colors: Gold and blue	**Flower**: Western red lily
Fish: Bull trout	**Grass**: Needle-and-thread grass
Flower: Wild rose	**Mammal**: White-tailed deer
Mammal: Rocky Mountain bighorn sheep	**Mineral**: Potash
Stone: Petrified wood	**Tree**: White birch
Tree: Lodgepole pine	**Sport**: Curling

Who determined the symbols for the provinces varied from symbol to symbol, year to year. In 1930, school children voted that the wild rose would be the flower symbol for Alberta. May 3rd, 1977, once again, Alberta children voted, this time choosing the Great Horned Owl as the bird to represent the province and the growing concern for diminishing wildlife. In fact, the range of the Great Horned Owl extends from Alaska to Mexico and includes all of Canada except north of the tree line. While visiting Kananaskis Country in about 1976, Calgary youth Mark Holt was fortunate to stand near the impressive bird. *Walt Holt Photo*

From Territories to Provinces

Generations of People

Generation after generation made its own contributions to the culture, priorities, and directions of the two provinces. First Nations people, explorers, map makers, traders, pioneer women, business people, educators, health providers, artists, sports heroes, and thousands of others all left their mark.

The many First Nations shared the landscape, as well as historical, cultural, and religious influences, but they had countless differences too. The major language groups were Algonkin, Athapaskan and Siouan. Powerful nations included the Cree, Blackfoot Confederation, Chipewyan, Beaver, Sarcee, and Slave. First Nations moved back and forth across what would become international and provincial boundaries. Yet, despite such similar early influences, each province gradually developed its own personality.

SOUIX INDIANS AT PRINCE ALBERT, SASK.

This Souix gathering was photographed at Prince Albert circa 1917. The Souix were one of the only First Nations groups that lived in Saskatchewan but were seldom found in Alberta. However, the related tribe, the Stoney, did live in Alberta. The most famous Souix visitor to the prairies was Sitting Bull who, along with about 5000 Lakota Souix, made the Wood Mountain area of Saskatchewan home from 1877 to 1886. *University of Saskatchewan Library, LXX-140*

The Mounties didn't just ride out to rescue the prairies from lawlessness. They rode into the history and symbolism of western Canada. They captured the hearts of maidens and helped settlers in isolated areas. They heroically fought prairie fires and crime. The Mounties, whether named NWMP, RNWMP or RCMP, added a dash of red to ceremonial occasions, including the inauguration of Alberta and Saskatchewan as provinces. Their impact was important in large and small communities, but nowhere more so than in Regina, which became the home of the RCMP training academy and museum. *Walt Holt Photo*

The wives of Mounted Police officers worked as partners with their husbands, especially in isolated communities. As very early settlers, these women witnessed the transformation of the prairies. That transformation included changes in fashions, child rearing practices, and home appliances. It also included dramatic shifts concerning the rights of prairie women. When Alberta and Saskatchewan women won the right to vote in 1916, most Mountie's wives would also be amongst the first female voters in Canada. *Saskatchewan Archives Board R-B 4311*

The Nault History

The Nault family history was tightly interwoven with the history of Alberta and Saskatchewan. The first Nault to move to the North-West Territories was born in Quebec, and he married a young woman born in the Cypress Hills area. By 1830, at St. Boniface [Manitoba], they had a son Andre [Sr.], who through his mother was a cousin of Riel. As a young man, Andre brought Riel to talk to surveyors who were measuring Nault land. There, Riel stood on the survey chain and ordered surveyors off the property. The event precipitated the Riel Rebellion, but Andre staunchly maintained it was not a rebellion, simply a response to injustice. The Métis wanted the right to make decisions about their own lands, and years later, in the North-West, that same issue would cause another confrontation.

By 1869, at age 39, Andre Nault [Sr.], became one of Riel's commanders and fought for Riel's beliefs. Andre helped seize Fort Garry, and in one instance, he was struck over the head with a rifle and left for dead. He survived but the depression in his skull remained. When all was lost, Andre and Riel fled to the USA, leaving the family behind and spending two years in exile. When Andre returned, he was imprisoned for another year, but his influence had spread. He was a hero to Métis, but his family of eleven children had moved even further west.

By 1879, his son Napoleon lived at Fort La Montee, formerly a North-West Company fort, [3rd Fort Carlton]. His brothers Andre, Jr., and Eli and their families had joined him. There, the hardworking brothers had a successful business, trading and freighting lumber and other supplies as far west as Edmonton.

Children of both Napoleon and Eli were born at Batoche, and through business and families, the Nault's influence continued to spread. Battleford, Prince Albert, and other communities along the Saskatchewan River routes had become homes for Naults.

When, once again, troubles surfaced for the Métis, Riel – second cousin of the young men – took over leadership. Becoming a Métis commander, Napoleon organized the sinking of the steamer Northcote. Then, following the battles of Batoche and Duck Lake, when all was lost, like his father, Napoleon fled to the USA, where he lived until his death.

By 1890, Eli and his family had moved to a homestead at nearby Jackfish Lake, and their story encompassed still other aspects of the western history. The family prospered, and within four years, they owned a herd of cattle. Wife

The Eli Nault family is shown here in 1905 at their farm at Jackfish Lake. Standing with 13 of their children, Eli is the tallest. Wife, Marie Anne, holds the baby. *Photo courtesy Ben Boutin*

Marie Anne nee Charette, whose Métis heritage spanned generations, gave birth to twenty-one children, fourteen of whom grew to adulthood.

Like other homesteaders, Eli "proved" his land. Then, to make extra money, he took ranch work elsewhere. His son, who had an adjacent farm, was to look after the property, but prairie fires were an ever-present danger. As was the case for thousands of settlers, one day, a fire burned across Eli's property and wiped out the homestead. By then, other settlers had arrived, so the family moved to more open territory.

Eventually, living at Midnight Lake, north of Battleford, life was filled with more joys and travesty. Their son Napoleon enlisted and died in the First World War. Their daughter died giving birth, so they raised the infant. In 1918, another son died of Spanish Flu. Still another son worked on the crew building the road to Meadow Lake. With sanitation conditions poor, contaminated water caused his death. Again and again, the extended Nault family was part of the prairie's history. They proved resilient and their descendants peopled both Alberta and Saskatchewan.

Fighting for What's Fair & Right

An important spokesperson in the late 1800s and early 1900s was Frederick Haultain. Born in England, he was premier of the North-West Territories from 1896 until 1905. He lobbied that the territory needed and was entitled to provincial status, with the same rights and responsibilities as the other provinces in Confederation.

The Districts of Assiniboia, Saskatchewan, Alberta, and Athabasca were destined to become the twin provinces.

The Territories encompassed everything west of Manitoba to the British Columbia border. A territorial council was elected and met in Regina to discuss relevant business, and it presented concerns to the Canadian government. While the needs were great, the population was small, and the voice of the West faint when compared to the rumblings of others. Sadly, federal funding was scant, and western power was limited.

A charismatic and charming man, most people in the west loved him. With a talent for administration and despite the mind of an expert politician, he gov-

Frederick Haultain *University of Saskatchewan Archives, A-2712*

To vote federally, prairie residents were sometimes casting ballots in nothing more than a tent pitched on the prairie. Shown here at Fort Qu'Appelle, North-West Territories, Federal Polling Station Number 75 was used for the election in 1904, one year before Alberta and Saskatchewan were granted provincial status. At the time, only white men were eligible voters. *Saskatchewan Archives Board R-B 1776*

erned according to his ethical values, and that meant doing what was right.

It was right that the west be allowed more self-government and direct control over local issues, an idea that was certainly not new. By 1901, with the Territories home to more than 165 500 people – far more than the 12 000 in Manitoba when it had become a province – the denial of such rights was more than irksome to a population continuing to grow. In addition, the federal government was not allocating money commensurate with the cost of essential services.

Haultain's plan called for one

huge province, which he named Buffalo. It would encompass land between Manitoba and British Columbia but extending only as far north as the Fort McMurray area.

With support from the Territorial Council, he presented the proposal to the federal government. Vague support turned to resistance. The government claimed there were other, bigger issues to solve. In fact, Manitoba was lobbying to extend her boundaries, and some Manitobans and provincial politicians believed she should annex part of the Territories.

Unlike other provinces, Manitoba didn't even have control over crown lands. That made her the poor sister of the other provinces. Rumblings in Manitoba were on the agenda before those in the Territories would be heard.

Haultain stood staunchly against annexation. The federal government had more objections and concerns related to schools and taxes, one of which was ensuring French in the Territories be guaranteed government-funded Catholic schools. Clearly, establishing new boundaries would be complicated.

By 1901, Prime Minister Laurier was definitely opposed to provincial status for the western territory. Supporters of provincial status, including Haultain, were not stopped in their tracks.

They presented five very different maps indicating where borders might be drawn:

- The two province plan, with the border running north and south;
- The two province plan with the border running east and west;
- The three province plan;
- The Manitoba plan; and
- The British Columbia plan.

The latter two added land to those provinces.

As premier of the Territories, Haultain had not allied himself with a political party. Then territorial voters decided to organize their own Conservative party. They asked Haultain to become honorary president. He accepted. Now he was on the opposite side, the wrong side, of Laurier and the federal Liberals. Not surprisingly, the face of political positioning raised its ugly head.

The wrangling continued. The Territories became increasingly insistent that provinces be carved out of the huge landscape. Finally, in 1905, Laurier's government conceded, welcoming Alberta and Saskatchewan into Confederation. Despite being the foremost warrior and commander in the battle for provincial status, and even with having the support of most westerners, Haultain lost out. He was a Conservative, and Laurier chose to appoint Liberals as the first premiers to the two new provinces.

Acts of Autonomy

Alberta & Saskatchewan Finally Provinces

The Canadian Parliament passed the Alberta Act and the Saskatchewan Act on July 20, 1905, but the two provinces did not official come into existence until September 1. With the exception of descriptions of geographical locations and the references to the temporary capital cities, the two acts were identical. Finally, the twins had a place of additional autonomy and self government in Canada's political landscape. Circumstances related to laws and the continuance of some regulations within the North-West Territories Act were identical in the two provincial acts. Terms were based on the assumption that each province had 250 000 people. In reality, populations in both areas were much smaller, but the high projection meant that financial terms were generous, suitable for a number of years, and were the same for both provinces. Both would receive $50 000 annually as a subsidy to support the government and legislature as well as $200 000, calculated at the rate of eight cents per person. When a census indicated that the population had grown beyond $250 000, the figure would be adjusted. Both would have four senators and twenty-five electoral division, with their specific geographical boundaries set out in each provincial act.

Canadian symbols were important in the celebrations of both Alberta and Saskatchewan. The Canadian coat of arms, Union Jack (official flag), and maple leaves donned the cover of the souvenir program for Edmonton in 1905. *Glenbow Archives, Calgary, Canada, NA 2318-17*

Special events in Edmonton and Regina were scheduled a few days apart so that Prime Minister Laurier and Canada's governor general could travel between the two cities and officiate at the celebrations of both provinces. Alberta held its ceremonies on September 1, 1905. Ceremonial events for Saskatchewan were scheduled for September 4th. The vice regal couple, Governor General and Lady Grey, are shown here alighting from a carriage in Regina's Victoria Square on September 4, 1905. *Saskatchewan Archives Board, R-A 2744*

Speeches, luncheons, balls, and sports events were featured during the inaugural celebrations in both Edmonton and Regina. Arches had been decorated in the downtown, and people enjoyed parades featuring First Nations, Mounties, bands, veterans, children, and local businesses. This photo shows women in the Edmonton parade. At the fair grounds, a 21-gun salute added to the solemnity of the occasion. *Glenbow Archives, Calgary, Canada, NA 1711-1*

Right Wing Alberta
Not Always Conservative

The first premier of Alberta was a Liberal, and the Alberta Liberal Party continued to form the government until 1921. Arriving in Edmonton South in 1895, Alexander Rutherford pursued a career in law and while he often adopted a nonpartisan approach to politics, by 1902, he was elected to the territorial government as a Liberal.

In 1905, he was appointed as Alberta's premier by Prime Minister Laurier and his Liberal government. In the province's first election, on November 9th, Rutherford proved he was the people's choice.

His party won 23 of the 25 seats in the new government. In 1909, he again won the election. By then, the legislature had 41 seats, and the Liberals held 37 of them. Under Arthur Sifton and Charles Stewart, Liberal governments remained in power until 1921. Alberta continued as a province of political dynasties, all of which had next to no opposition in the legislature. The United Farmers of Alberta ruled from 1921 to 1935. Social Credit held office for 36 years from 1935 to 1971, when power moved to the Conservative dynasty.

On the left is George Bulyea, the province's first lieutenant governor. In the middle is Donald A. Smith, who was instrumental in the building of the CPR, and was later named Lord Strathcona. On the right, is Alberta's first premier, Alexander Cameron Rutherford. *City of Edmonton Archives, EA 10-1669*

From Penniless Waif to Premier

Premier Walter Scott
Saskatchewan Archives Board R-A 3200

As a young man, Walter Scott moved to the District of Saskatchewan from his birthplace in Ontario. His early life had been hard; his father had died before Scott was born in 1867, and by eleven years of age, Scott was working in the summer, earning 15 cents a day, haying and harvesting. By age fourteen, he had stayed with an uncle much of the time. The uncle was, among other things, a school teacher, but Scott's schooling was brief and interrupt-

ed. Because he was an asthmatic, the dry, clear air of the west was prescribed as an antidote. So, at the age of seventeen, he convinced his mother he should go west to the home of another uncle at Portage la Prairie, Manitoba. Once there, his farming career did not work out.

In 1885, he took a four-year apprenticeship at a printing office, where his position was referred to as "devil." Initially, he had menial duties such as cleaning, starting fires, and running errands. Before the year was up, he was typesetting. When staff was short, he would pull an all-nighter but work the next day as well. Not surprisingly, his boss recognized his work ethic and the quality of his work, including his contributions as a reporter. In 1886, Scott was transferred to his bosses newly-acquired publishing venture in Regina.

Despite the promotion, money was a problem. Scott's salary was $5.50 a week and board was $5. He was given a raise of $1 per week, an increase he badly needed. Becoming correspondent for the *Winnipeg Free Press* put an extra $2 per week in his pocket.

Eventually, Scott's interests turned to politics. He changed jobs and began working for *The Leader*, the principle newspaper in Regina and the west. Later, he worked for *The Standard* but changed papers again, moved to Winnipeg, then back to Regina. Though now married, he found himself almost penniless. While back working at *The Standard*, he and a friend decided to buy it, so they borrowed money and took out mortgages. Two years later, in 1894, Scott purchased the *Moose Jaw Times* at a bankruptcy sale. Eventually, his businesses took off, and Scott managed to purchase *The Leader*. Unfortunately ,here were political strings attached to the purchase, numer-

ous unusual clauses in the agreement, and other problems with the sale and ownership of the paper.

Despite the troubles, with Scott's editorials about territorial government, the paper's and his own reputation grew. Eventually, the Liberal party in the west had him handling numerous responsibilities, including controversial patronage issues. By 1900, his time had come.

In the midst of controversy and challenges, he won in the federal election. Scott was Member of Parliament for West Assiniboia. Five years later, with the passage of the Saskatchewan Act in 1905, he was appointed as Saskatchewan's first premier.

The first provincial election was slated for December 13 of that year. Scott ran against Haultain, former premier of the North-West Territories and a Conservative. Despite the renown of Haultain, Scott won.

He remained in power until 1916 when ill health forced him to retire. Liberals continued to govern Saskatchewan until 1929. From then until 1934, Conservatives were at the helm. Next came ten more years of Liberal rule prior to the CCF/NDP becoming significant in provincial elections between 1944 and 1964. Then the story began again: Liberals, NDP and then Conservatives.

Saskatchewan: Starting Over

Photographed in 1919, the site for the Regina Legislative Building was on the south side of Wascana Lake. *City of Regina Archives, CORA-RPL-A-755*

Regina had been home to the Legislative Assembly of the North-West Territories, and in 1905, its building became the site of the new Saskatchewan government. For the growing province, the building was too small and a new one needed to be built.

Wascana Lake was the water reservoir for the city, built by the federal government and CPR by damming Wascana Creek. The shore of the lake was park-like and perfect for the new building.

Construction began in 1908, with marble the preferred material. Although limestone from Manitoba was to face the building, thirty-four types of marble were imported from as far away as Cypress and Ireland. This was used for everything from walls and staircases, to baseboards and pillars.

By 1910, some offices were in operation, and by January, 1912, the legislature met in the building for the first time, though the session had to be held in the library.

Then, in June, the Regina tornado hit. Damage to the structure was minor but still necessitated repairs. Finally, in October of that year, with pomp and ceremony, Governor General Connaught, son of Queen Victoria, and his daughter, Princess Patricia, officially opened the new site. Although the building was now the seat of the provincial legislature, significant work was still being done on it and the grounds. In 1913, 11 000 trees and shrubs were planted on the grounds. At completion in 1919, the total cost had mounted from the 1912 estimate of $1.8 million to $3 million.

Alberta: Building From Scratch

This unique photo of Alberta's Legislative Building was taken in 1914 from the road that ran under the High Level Bridge. *Glenbow Archives, Calgary, Canada, NC-6-1091*

Edmonton did not have an old government building where it could hold the first session of the Alberta legislature, nor did it have traditional symbols, but the newly appointed premier knew the importance of symbols. In British tradition, lawmakers required a mace, so before the first sitting of the legislature, one had to be crafted. The job went to Rufus Butterworth, a CPR employee living in Calgary. Like any good pioneer, he used materials at hand. A plumbing pipe made a shaft; for the top, he used a bulbous float from the toilet-tanks of the day. Wood scraps, shaving mug handles, and metal scraps from a bedstead were also used. When everything was in place, Butterworth added velvet and painted his creation gold. It looked just like– or almost like – a mace, and was used to open the first legislative session in Alberta.

On March 15, 1906, legislature met in the Thistle Roller and Ice Rink. The first session lasted only an hour, but 4 000 attended to witness the event.

Construction began on an ornate, domed building in 1907. For the exterior, sandstone was shipped from Calgary and Ohio, and granite from Vancouver Island. The interior marble came from Pennsylvania and Quebec.

The Legislative Building opened in September, 1912, and Governor General Connaught officiated. The first mace served Alberta well, but for the province's 50th birthday in 1955, a mace of real silver, gold, and jewels was crafted. The original remains a treasured reminder of the past.

Drawn to the Possibilities

The Rush of Settlers & Scarcity of Homes

Some settlers journeyed to the prairies by wagon all the way from eastern Canada or the United States. Most travelled by rail to a large community and then by wagon to their homesteads. This couple was setting out from Moose Jaw, SK, for their homestead. *Saskatchewan Archives Board, R-B-3386*

Between 1901 and 1906, the population of rural and urban areas of the prairie provinces grew dramatically. Calgary's population mushroomed from about 4 100 to almost 12 000. Edmonton went from about 2 600 to about 11 500. The boom continued. In 1906, Regina had a population of 6 070. By 1911, the city was home to 30 213 people.

The housing crunch hit hard in towns and cities, and many homesteaders were surprised to find no houses on their land. Worse yet, in areas with few trees, building materials were limited. Buying "catalogue" homes was expensive but so was hauling building materials from the nearest store and railway.

Out of necessity, on the treeless southern prairies, soddies became an answer to the housing problem. The style of the earthen houses was dependent on the building skills of the home owners but also on how scarce lumber was. Some homes were made almost entirely of sod. Others were a combination of materials. They might have wood frames and sod walls, or lumber frame, walls, and roof but sod around the exterior as insulation. Inside, women were innovative, using sheets, tar paper, or wall paper hung from the "ceiling" as wall coverings or room dividers. Some shelters had windows and others had none.

The first home for these Saskatchewan settlers was a make-shift tent-like shelter. *Saskatchewan Archives Board, R-A 2335*

Adapting to sod or shack homes was often difficult and pioneers did as much of their work as possible outside, including churning butter and washing clothes. The response of women to their odd prairie homes was as varied as the women themselves. Years later, some would fondly remember the soddies, despite roofs dripping for days after heavy rains. *Glenbow Archives, Calgary, Canada, NA 1789-3*

Two Ministers, Two Provinces, One City

The history and life of one town truly exemplifies the twin "lives" – the dualities and the differences – of Saskatchewan and Alberta. Founded just before provincial status was granted, Lloydminster was based on a utopian plan. The vision was to settle English farmers in a land of milk and honey, and to ensure western Canada remained British.

In 1902, Reverend Isaac Barr, an Ontario-born Anglican clergyman ministering in England, came up with the idea and began recruiting. By 1903, the group had grown to about 2 000 and included a second minister, Reverend George Lloyd, who became the settlers' chaplin. When the colonists left Liverpool, one of the ships carried almost double the passengers it had been designed to accommodate. While Reverend Barr did paperwork in his cabin, Reverend Lloyd ministered to the sick on the voyage. To some, Barr was no longer a knight in shining armor.

Once in Canada, the settlers travelled by train to Saskatoon. Not expecting the basic conditions of the railway cars, colonists suffered from the below zero March weather, and more of the them were disillusioned.

Even so, many Barr colonists arrived still filled with hope and anticipating productive farms by fall. Then the utopian plan became mired in trouble. At Saskatoon, the newcomers planned to set up a temporary camp. Having paid Barr

Barr colonists spent about two weeks camped near the railway tracks in Saskatoon.
Saskatoon Public Library, LH 1352

in advance for tents and water-proof groundsheets, they expected them on arrival. Where were the tents? Some had been packed on later trains. Others were nowhere to be found. Had Barr simply taken their money? It was a bad start.

The single immigration hall could hold very few. Fortunately, the Canadian government came to the rescue with tents used by troops in the South African War. There were only a few outdoor toilets for the colonists to use, and although the days were warm, the nights were cold. For water, they melted river ice. Again, disillusionment rose as colonists readied themselves for homestead life.

There were no stores near the homesteads, and prices in Saskatoon were high for necessities. The price for horses and oxen was outrageous. With the unexpected expenses, some families were destitute, and men took whatever jobs they could find wherever they could find them. Again, to many, Barr was to blame for not warning them.

Some headed out for Rosthern, fifty miles away, where prices were rumored to be lower. Others paid the asking price in Saskatoon. Acrimony and intrigue increased. Barr was considered the villain, and the group appointed Reverend Lloyd as the new leader. After all, he had both the organizational and people skills.

By the time settlers left Saskatoon, they had purchased 500 wagons, 1 000 horses, 800 ploughs, other tools, groceries, and household items, but many weren't properly clothed for the weather.

At their new homesteads, many of the Barr colonists continued to live in their tents until fall or even spring. *Saskatchewan Archives Board, R-B 2764-1*

For the 180 mile trip, they started at daybreak and struggled through boggy land. Wagon wheels broke on the rough trails, crossing creeks, and travelling steep hills. The problems seemed endless.

Finally, some homesteaders got settled, but Reverend Lloyd and about 500 others chose to found their own village, which they named Lloydminster. Then in 1905, once again, life became complicated for the group.

The provincial border ran through the middle of town. Part was in Alberta while the larger area was in Saskatchewan, and nothing was easy. In terms of paperwork, cost of services, and bureaucracy, the town did double duty. The Alberta village of Lloydminster elected a mayor, and the town of Lloydminster on the Saskatchewan side also elected a mayor. There were two town councils, two police forces, and two fire departments.

The duplication became ridiculous, and representatives approached both provincial governments for a resolution. Finally, in May of 1930, both provinces passed the Lloydminster Municipal Amalgamation Act. The town was now united and became Lloydminster, Saskatchewan-Alberta.

The twin cities were adjacent to each other but each had a different corporate identity, and Lloydminster received political and legal recognition in both provinces.

Legislation made sense: one mayor, town council, police department and fire department, but government-related paper work was still doubled. Provincial programs in one province did not apply in the other.

There were additional oddities as well. Originally, Lloydminster, Alberta, had a smaller population, but growth on the Alberta side outpaced growth on the Saskatchewan side, despite housing being more expensive on the Alberta side.

Saskatchewan had the exhibition grounds and the golf and country club, but Lloydminster's Lakeland College was built in Alberta. Today, the oddities continue. On the Alberta side, liquor is cheaper, and eighteen-year-olds have the right to drink. In Lloydminster, Saskatchewan, teens must be nineteen to drink. Saskatchewan residents have a higher minimum wage and are entitled to more weeks of vacation, but they have a sales tax. Albertans don't have a provincial sales tax, but they do pay a health care premium. Saskatchewan citizens don't pay the premiums, but they have the hospital cost. The bi-provincial city is certainly unique, and descendants of the Barr colonists and the thousands of others who have joined them love it.

Diverse Beliefs

Spreading Christianity to First Nations populations was a priority for early missionaries, especially Roman Catholics, but the Canadian west was chosen by some religious groups because it offered freedom of religion. Doukhobors, Mennonites, Mormons, and Hutterites were among them. When large numbers of a particular religious group settled in an area, often others of the same ethnic and religious background gravitated to the same location. Extended family and groups of friends chose to live near each other.

Building churches was a high priority, not only in the towns but in rural areas. Churches were built in the middle of seemingly uninhabited prairies. Often they were an indication of the ethnicity and religious following of the surrounding population.

Greek Orthodox and Ukranian Orthodox settlers built dome-like churches. Commonly, they are found in and near communities such as Edmonton and Vegreville in Alberta. Others were built north of Saskatoon and in east-central Saskatchewan. *Saskatchewan Archives Board, Melville-Ness Photo, S-MN-B 1408*

Communal Settlers in the West

The Doukhobors, the Christian Community of Universal Brotherhood, were among the earliest settlers to seek religious freedom in western Canada. The movement of the sect across provincial borders was one of the many ways in which the history of the two provinces was interrelated.

Pacifism, independence from the Orthodox Church, freedom from nationalism, rational living, and communal farming were fundamentals for Doukhobors. Suffering persecution in Russia, more than 7 000 came to western Canada, and between 1889 to 1899, they settled in the general area of Yorkton, Saskatchewan.

Conflict was not so easy to escape. They were hard working farmers, but the relationship

To fulfill their dream for a better life, in about 1905, these Doukhobor women labored to sod the roof of this home in Saskatchewan. Many Doukhobor men took wage earning jobs in the Prince Albert area to earn much needed cash. *British Columbia Archives and Records Service, E-09610*

between them and officials was rocky.

Although they farmed communally, they were required to apply individually for homesteads. When the time arrived to swear oaths of allegiance and be granted title to the homesteads, the crisis came to a head. Removing their clothes and parading was a method of peaceful protest for the Doukhobors, but it was not a politically acceptable one, and many were imprisoned. Without the required oaths of allegiance, the government cancelled their homestead applications.

Saskatchewan appeared not to be the perfect land for them, and leader Peter Verigin (Peter the Lordly) led many of them away.

In 1908, under his leadership, about 6 000 sect members moved to BC. Then in 1915, Verigin decided an Alberta sect was needed to provide grain and flour for the much larger BC colony, and about 300 people moved to Alberta. The communal farmers held approximately 1 200 acres of farmland in the Cowley-Lunbreck area, and the BC colony supplied them with fruit and garden vegetables.

Verigin frequently travelled back and forth among the communities. In 1924, as he made one of his many train trips from Alberta

to BC, an explosion ripped the air in the railway car. Verigin was dead.

Anastasia Holuboff, the companion who had lived and travelled with Verigin for more than twenty years, wanted leadership but was defeated. Instead, the Doukhobors chose Verigin's son, also named Peter. By 1927, he had moved from Russia to Canada.

Increasingly, the Alberta Doukhobors became independent farmers, but Anastasia established her own splinter group. When she lost the leadership, she moved with them to the outskirts of Calgary and purchased 1 120 acres in her own name. At its peak, her sect included 165 people from twenty-six households, but Anastasia never signed the lands over to the community.

A rigid leader, she made her group sign pledges prohibiting firearms, killing animals for food, using alcohol, smoking, and chewing tobacco. She delivered diatribes at wrongdoers, and given the constant infighting, many left the colony with only the clothes on their backs. By 1945, only Anastasia and a companion remained in her village. They abandoned it in 1960 and moved to Calgary where Anastasia died five years later.

Enriching Our Cultural Mosaic

Chinese men were among the many immigrants settling on the west coast. Many worked on the Canadian Pacific Railway line from the coast through the Rockies. Later they moved east to the prairies and worked as cooks for families or in cafes, or opened their own restaurants and laundries. In later years, as racial obstacles lifted, they entered all professions. These men are dressed for the 1935 Edmonton Exhibition parade. Chinese women did not have the same opportunity to immigrate to Canada. According to the 1921 Canadian Census, Edmonton was home to 501 Chinese men but only 17 Chinese women. *Glenbow Archives, Calgary, Canada, NA 3976-2*

In Saskatchewan, black pioneers settled in the Weyburn and Prince Albert areas. By the early 1900s, a large community had also settled in Alberta. Many who went to Amber Valley and other small communities north of Edmonton were from Oklahoma. This 1930s baseball team was from Amber Valley. *Glenbow Archives, Calgary, Canada, NA 704-6*

From Agriculture to Agribusiness

Homesteads for Newcomers

The job of plowing or braking the land was captured for this post card. The spelling on the hand written note would not have affected the recipient's understanding nor the homesteader's ability to do the job. *University of Saskatchewan Library, SPC-pamphlets, box 252-Braking*

Thousands of early settlers came to Alberta and Saskatchewan lured by the agricultural potential and the opportunity to own land by homesteading it. A head of household, including women, could apply for a homestead of 160 acres. All the applicant needed to do was pay a small registration fee of $10, live on the property at least six months a year, and cultivate the land. Not surprisingly, there was competition for the homesteads. At land offices, people were prepared to wait in line for days when an area was to be opened.

An adjacent quarter section could also be preempted, and once the homesteader was granted title to the initial quarter, he or she could pay $2.50 per acre for the pre-empted land. The price was based on the CPR land for sale to new settlers. Also, numerous colonization companies had secured large land grants to put up for sale. However, homestead land was virtually free.

By the beginning of the 20th Century, most who came to the North-West Territory districts were intent on farming. Soon, much of the land between the fringe area of heavy forest in the north and the southern border was ploughed, and fields were sown. Some discovered their homesteads were in semi arid desert, but at first, little could defeat their dreams.

Before long, Saskatchewan had more land devoted to agricultural uses than any other province in Canada. The province could boast that its farm land exceeded the combined total of agricultural land in Alberta and Manitoba.

Yet in all three provinces, farming was big business. Historically, in Saskatchewan, about 60 percent of the crop was wheat. In 1906, the average price of that wheat was 77 cents a bushel; in 1910, it rose to $1.10, and then prices began to fluctuate. By 1919, farmers could expect about $2.32, but prices varied according to grade, time of year, and method of

No matter how small the farm or expensive and large the tractors, farming required hard working people. For decades, thousands of itinerant harvesters came west to work at the harvest, but in the years before giant combines, within communities, a co-operative approach at harvest time was the norm.
Provincial Archives of Alberta 541

marketing. Eighty-five years later, in 2004, wheat was about $3.50 a bushel at port, little more than three times its 1910 value. In contrast, the price of leather work boots in the Hudson Bay catalogue of 1910-1911 ranged from $1.25 to $3.75. Today's work boots at the Bay are from $130 to $170, or about ten times the minimum price in 1910. No longer can one bushel of wheat purchase a pair of boots.

Largely due to mechanization, the size of farms increased. Tractors and large threshing machines were in demand. Yet by 1964, only 36 large machine shops and 13 other establishments manufactured agricultural implements in Saskatchewan. The situation was similar in Alberta, but both provinces were home to men who patented numerous agricultural inventions. They designed their own ploughs, root harrows, discs, attachments for seed grain drills, weeders, threshing machines and attachments, and the Noble blade, which prevented soil erosion. However, most agricultural equipment was shipped by rail to western Canada, and freight costs became an issue for farmers. Still, the annual delivery of equipment always attracted interested farmers, as shown here on Stettler's Main Street in 1908. *Glenbow Archives, Calgary, Canada, NA 1497-56*

No Rain, No Grain

Explorer John Palliser cautioned that desert-like conditions made the land that would become southeast Alberta and southwest Saskatchewan unfit for agriculture. To ensure productivity, the CPR dammed the Bow River for irrigation. In 1910, construction began on the Bassano Dam, but workers also had to build aqueducts, canals, flumes, syphons, spillways, and dozens of other components. By 1914, most of the work was done to launch the Eastern District of the CPR Irrigation Project, and large-scale irrigation began to change the face of southern Alberta.

The railway company continued to expand the system, and south of Brooks, it created Lake Newell, the largest man-made lake in Alberta. In 1935, the CPR transferred ownership of the irrigation system to farmers and ranchers. Now named the Eastern Irrigation District (EID), the system served close to 1 000 000 acres of land. Most shares were held by individuals, but some was under the collective ownership of the EID.

By 2004, the EID irrigated the largest area of any irrigation system in the province. Twelve additional irrigation districts had been created in Alberta. The Western Irrigation District, which served the Strathmore area south to Gleichen and north to near Airdrie, was the second largest.

Prior to pouring concrete for the spillway sill, workers on the Bassano Dam assembled the framework. *Eastern Irrigation District Archives, B 3497*

Irrigation did not play a significant role in Saskatchewan, mostly because few major rivers or bodies of water were in the semi-arid area to provide the needed water. By 1966, only 722 farms in Saskatchewan were irrigated. The water for the system was supplied by Diefenbaker Lake, which was created by building a dam on the South Saskatchewan River near Saskatoon.

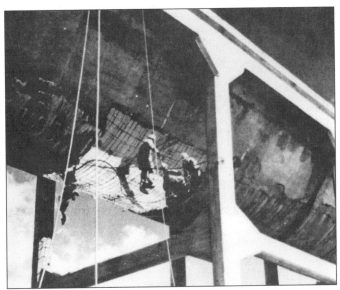

To do repairs to the aqueduct bowl, one man stands on the rebar, visible through the hole. His co-workers are on the edge of the hole. Repairs were only a small part of the work of the EID, which has offices in Brooks, Alberta. *Eastern Irrigation District Archives, B 3008B*

Taken in 1913, this work gang rests in the bowl of the aqueduct, which is under construction. The shell is more than 6.4 metres (21 feet wide), and the bowl will be more than 2.4 metres (8 feet) deep. *Eastern Irrigation District Archives, B 3003*

Elevators:

Service, Sentinels and Symbols

University of Saskatchewan Archives, Wheat Pool (MG 247), Series 10, Slide Tape Project, 28, Grain Growers

Early grain farmers faced countless difficulties, including marketing grain. Until the development of the elevator system, grain was sacked, and wagonloads were hauled to the railway. Railways and private elevator companies called the shots. The companies had built storage facilities near the railways and had preferential treatment. Small-scale farmers could not fill a car on their own, so they were forced to wait with their grain or sell it to the private companies at rock bottom prices. Without adequate storage facilities of their own, farmers simply couldn't wait around for better prices.

Prior to 1905, the North-West Grain Dealers Association and the Territorial Grain Growers Association tackled the issues for western farmers. As a result, in 1897, a fixed rate for shipping grain was established. Called the Crow Rate, it remained in existence until 1996. But problems went even deeper.

By 1906, the associations had been reorganized by province. Both the Saskatchewan Grain Growers Association (SGGA) and the Alberta association continued to advocate that farmers could do better building their own elevators for storage and marketing grain through a co-operative.

Like railway stations, new elevators were built about every eight to ten miles along the railway so that farmers had ready access to them. Although the first elevators were varied in shape, the exact dimensions of the primary elevators were established in 1913, and so important were the elevators, groupings of them helped determine the location of towns.

These primary elevators became sentinels, landmarks, and symbols to prairie people, but larger grain terminals were also erected. In Alberta, they were built at Edmonton, Calgary and Lethbridge. Similar ones were constructed in Saskatoon and Moose Jaw.

In Alberta, by 1917, the provincial Grain Growers Company and the Alberta Farmer's Co-operative

The Grain Pool Elevator at Wetaskiwin, Alberta, was under construction June 13, 1928. *City of Wetaskiwin Archives, Carl W. Walin Photo, Carl W. Walin fonds, 98.37-28-152*

Sacks of grain weighed about 54 kg (120 pounds) each. Loading them into railway cars was time consuming, and hard work. *Saskatchewan Archives Board, R-B 10127*

Elevator Company merged as the United Grain Growers, precursor to the UFA. Although company names changed, collective grain marketing companies received phenomenal support. Despite the periodic furor by the Winnipeg Grain Exchange, even Alberta and Saskatchewan legislation supported the elevator and marketing system.

Organized in 1923, the Alberta Wheat Pool garnered contracts that pooled 35 percent of the grain acreage in the province. When the Saskatchewan Wheat Pool was established in 1924, it won wheat delivery contracts from 45 725 of the province's farmers, and Mani-

toba had also formed a Pool. Uniting as the Canadian Co-operative Wheat Producers Ltd., they became the central selling agency for grain. Acquiring elevators and terminals, the Wheat Pool became a force for western farmers.

Federal involvement in grain marketing was most apparent in 1919. As a war measure, Canada established the Wheat Board. It lasted only a year, but ten years later, with the stock market crash, the federal government was again involved in marketing. The Wheat Pools were failing and the government bailed them out, acquiring their assets and their unsold grain. By 1935, Canada had established

In its heyday, Vulcan, Alberta, elevators shipped more grain directly from farms by rail to 35 000 bushels, and each could fill about 10 railcars a day. Of the elevators at Vulcan, seven In Alberta alone, during the 1930s, 1 755 elevators were in operation. *Glenbow Archives,*

the Government Marketing Board, and with WW II, it handed over a monopoly in grain marketing to the re-established Canadian Wheat Board.

Fifty years later, many farmers were adamantly opposed to that monopoly. Some westerners insisted that both the Wheat Board and Wheat Pool had failed them. By the year 2000, the government-owned Pool had a debt of $1 billion. Employees were cut, and elevators were being closed. By 2003, the once mighty Wheat Pool faced bankruptcy.

Today, Agricore has become the big player in the grain handling system, but with improved communications, Internet marketing and international trucking possibilities, some farmers want to do their own marketing. Prepared to defy the law, they want to truck grain across the border where the prices are higher. Some farmers will even face jail for the freedom to sell their own grain. The controversies over grain marketing continue. But almost all farmers lament the loss of the great sentinels of the prairies.

markets than anywhere else in the British Empire. By 1913, most elevators had a capacity of
were nonstandard, double capacity elevators. The larger elevators could fill 50 rail cars a day
Calgary, Canada PA 3369, Vulcan 14

David Hamilton photographed this spectacular multi-elevator fire light up the night and rage out of control at Kyle, SK, in August, 1981. The lumber construction, huge capacity for storage of grain to fuel a fire, and dusty conditions made the grain elevators highly flammable. Given the height of the prairie sentinels, the fires were impossible to effectively fight. *University of Saskatchewan, Saskatchewan Wheat Pool, David Hamilton Photo, MG 247, Series 10, Elevators, Folder 1. Box 141*

By 1975, when this Bratton Elevator was being moved to Delisle, Saskatchewan, some small elevators had been closed or torn down. Rail lines were being abandoned and railways wanted to sell the company-owned land where many elevators stood. Railways gave incentives to elevator companies when they required fewer stops. Large terminals with computerized systems had become more cost effective. With elevators closing in both Alberta and Saskatchewan, farmers, townspeople, and various heritage groups offered to buy elevators and move them if necessary, but they were fighting a losing battle. *Saskatchewan Archives Board, Saskatoon, Rusty Mac-Donald Photo, S-RM-A 1062*

Closure and demolition of elevators accelerated after the late 1960s. In 1995, the Wheat Pool closed 100 elevators on the prairies over the next three years. By 1998, another 170 elevators were destroyed. In 2000, 63 more were closed. By then, Alberta had 209 remaining elevators, and Saskatchewan had been equally decimated. Photographed by Paul Boorah, the demolition of Herbert, Saskatchewan grain elevator took place in 1979. *University of Saskatchewan Archives, Saskatchewan Wheat Pool, Paul Boorah Photo, MG 247, Series 10, Elevators, Folder 1, Box 141, Herbert, SK, 3*

When the Herbert elevator crashed to the ground, dust and debris filled the air. In countless prairie communities, similar scenes had broken the hearts of those who wanted save a way of life, a symbol, and a heritage. *University of Saskatchewan Archives, Saskatchewan Wheat Pool, Paul Boorah Photo, MG 247, Series 10, Elevators, Folder 1, Box 141, Herbert, SK, 11*

The Business of Cattle

In the late 1800s, ranching in southern Saskatchewan and Alberta meant grazing thousands of cattle, and ranchers depended on vast tracts of pasture acquired at very little cost. In the south and west, soil conditions and lack of precipitation made land little-suited to grain farming. Also, in the foothills, forestry reserve land could be leased as pasture.

Mixed farms predominated in central areas of the provinces, but there was a brisk business in cattle, and beef production continued to flourish. Between 1906 and 1913, the number of cattle, including dairy, more than doubled in Saskatchewan, but the cattle industry was even more important to the agricultural economy of Alberta.

Feed for livestock, especially where minimal winter grazing was possible, meant hay production was also important. Periodically, shortages of hay and feed threatened the industry.

In 2002, prairie farmers were desperate for feed. Fellow farmers from eastern Canada sent hay by rail to Alberta and some areas of Saskatchewan. Hay lotteries were anxiously attended. Unfortunately, some hay was infested with cereal beetles, and the time required for fumigating caused shipment delays. Delays led to mould, and farmers remained desperate. Some Alberta farmers even explored the possibility of pasturing cattle in those areas of Saskatchewan not as hard-hit by the drought.

The problem was immense, but proved not to be the worst of their predicaments. Instead, bovine spongiform encephalopathy (BSE) would devastate a once thriving beef industry.

With machines such as this over stacker, operated near Red Deer, one man and a tractor could handle more of the work on farms and ranches. *Glenbow Archives, Calgary, Canada, NA 4172-23*

In 1912, ranchers then, as now, were watchful for problems. Here cattle are herded through a dip to treat them for mange, a parasitic mite causing skin irritations and lesions. Fairly common in Alberta, it affected the animals' general condition and appearance but never led to the devastation of BSE, mad cow disease. In May of 2003, markets plummeted when a slaughtered animal in Alberta was found to have BSE. With Alberta's testing facilities overtaxed and understaffed, discovery of the problem had been delayed, but immediately, inspectors traced the source and any possible spread of the disease. Americans closed their border to Canadian cattle, and

despite no further cases being discovered, negotiations to reopen the border remained futile. Since the USA was the primary market for Canadian cattle, the closure crippled the industry. Ranchers were on the brink of despair and bankruptcy. Federal and provincial programs were implemented to help beef producers, but they set time-lines for the sale of cattle in order for producers to collect. Producers were forced to flood the market, and the winners were meat packers, who picked up huge herds of cattle at low prices. Because feedlot operators now owned large herds, two packing plant companies collected about 11 percent of the money available for assistance. While packers tripled their usual profits, many beef producers went out of business. *Brooks Museum P06 - 17*

In Saskatchewan by 1906, milk cows comprised 23 percent of cattle. By 1913, that had risen to 38 percent. Often, women were responsible for milking, separating cream and milk, and making butter. Many farmers sold milk privately or hauled it to dairies or creameries. The first pasteurized milk in Alberta was available in the spring of 1906. Door-to-door delivery was common, and a horse-drawn milk wagon was used in Edmonton as late as 1961. *University of Saskatchewan Archives, Livestock, L, Separating Milk*

Building Towns & Community

Endless Essential Services

The growing populations of the twin provinces meant an increasing need in villages, towns, and cities for houses, banks, bakeries, and laundries. They had to have hardware, grocery, and clothing stores as well as equipment dealerships and blacksmiths. The children needed schools and everyone required health services. Sidewalks, roads, and sewage systems had to be provided. The growth offered opportunities for professionals and experienced trades people, but also created jobs for young and old, married and unmarried, men and women of all skill levels.

When so much of the culture on the prairies was based on horses, blacksmith shops, such as this one at Innisfail, Alberta, were some of the first businesses to be established in towns. However, shaping horseshoes was only one of their many jobs and they repaired countless items made of medal. *Glenbow Archives, Calgary, Canada, NA 1709-52*

Stone masons were important tradesmen. The CPR used stone for many of its early structures, and Calgary became the Sandstone City because of the use of sandstone for city buildings after the devastating fire of 1886. This stone mason was employed in the construction of a building at the University of Saskatchewan building. *University of Saskatchewan Archives A 877-2*

Before the turn of the century, in the district of Alberta, many stone quarries had been established including on the Elbow River, as well as near Cochrane, Red Deer, and Bowden. Other quarries were built in Castor and Exshaw, where limestone was also quarried. In about 1912, this quarry company operated about 6 miles north-west of Monarch, AB. Between 1910 and 1913, 60 Scottish stone masons were employed there, and the quarried stone was used as close by as Lethbridge and as far away as Banff. *Glenbow Archives, Calgary, Canada, NA 3267*

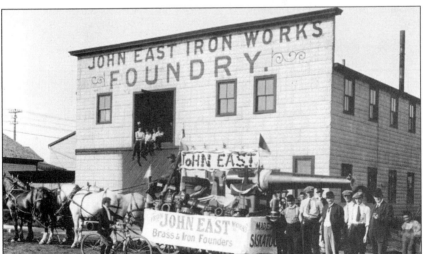

Iron foundries were important to the construction industry. Buildings were larger and higher, and bridges needed to be built to span great rivers. Early irrigation systems in Alberta required specialized steel constructions, as did mining, boat building, and petroleum industries. Here, Saskatoon's John East Brass and Iron Founders have mounted a cannon and other equipment for a float in the annual parade. *Saskatoon Public Library LH LH 3986*

Early Health Care Providers

Hospitals were necessities. Early on, large communities had hospital beds and accommodated surgery. In small communities, as late as the fourth decade of the 19th Century, often, local doctors had a bed or two in their homes to monitor patient recovery. Such personal care continued much later in northern communities.

However, public responsibility for health care was already taking root in Saskatchewan when Saskatoon opened the first municipally owned hospital in western Canada in 1909. In other communities, too, lobbying for free provincial hospitals began very early.

In rural Alberta in 1916, Irene Parlby, President of the United Farm Women of Alberta, and her organization lobbied for free hospitals and district nursing. In Calgary, Maude Riley, convener of laws for Calgary Local Council of Women urged government fund-

Sophisticated peddlars, offering patent "medicines," travelled door to door in rural areas but they also took their wares to local fairs. They used all manner of promotional gimmicks to promote the health benefits of their products. This group of "snake oil salesmen" at a Saskatchewan fair linked their product to the indigenous people. *Courtesy of the Saskatchewan Archives Board, R-A 18798*

ing for municipal hospitals.

At the same time, Violet McNaughton in Saskatchewan, along with the Women's Grain Growers Association, campaigned relentlessly for government supported medical services and hospitals. McNaughton both spoke and wrote about desperate health conditions. In a speech to the group, quoting from 1914 Saskatchewan hospital statistics, she indicated one woman in three suffered injury during maternity because of inadequate or inappropriate medical treatment.

Of the 17 282 births in the province that year, 1 637 – almost 1 in 10 – of the children died before their fifth birthday. To women's groups, free treatment was not a privilege but a right.

In about 1896, Dr. Frank Mewburn, the hospital matron, nurses, and housekeeper posed for their photos in the operating room at the Galt Hospital at Lethbridge, Alberta. Because they owned a coal mining company and injuries were a serious risk, the Galt family had built a private hospital. *Sir Alexander Galt Museum & Archives, Lethbridge, P19737730000-GP*

Waterworks, Sanitation, & Sewers

For water, some towns could depend on nearby rivers. Others drilled wells. Water towers were erected for storage and to create a pressure system. At first, outhouses were the norm, but soon, sewers were high on the agenda of most towns. Home owners at the outskirts of towns and on farms continued to pump water and use outhouses. In northern areas and on isolated farms, indoor plumbing did not become reasonably universal until well after WW II. Here Red Deer workers are installing pipe for a sewer system in 1905. *Red Deer Archives, Mg-26-1-10*

In 1907, Regina had 11.7 km (7.25 miles) of sewers and the small town of Prince Albert, Saskatchewan, home to slightly more than 3 000 people, had no sidewalks but had constructed 6.4 km (4 miles) of water mains. By 1911, both communities had more than tripled their sewer lines. *City of Regina Archives,CORA-B-493*

Fire Protection

In 1904, Saskatoon purchased a pumper, its first piece of fire fighting equipment. Shown here in 1911, it was pulled by oxen. Standing in the background is Princess School. *Saskatoon Public Library, LH 1209*

The Calgary Fire Department began as a volunteer brigade called the Calgary Hook, Ladder, and Bucket Corps. The "volunteers" were paid 75 cents for each fire they attended. Perhaps the most notorious captain was James "Cappy" Smart, who joined the brigade in 1885 and became fire chief in 1898. Serving until 1933, he saw the department grow from wagons and horses to numerous motor vehicles. In 1910, the first truck was nicknamed "the buzz-wagon," and it carried both the squad and a chemical tank. The vehicle was capable of 64 kmh (40 mph) when the speed limit was only 32 kmh (20 mph) in the city. Shown here in 1912, Calgary's Fire Department claimed to be the first fully mechanized one in Canada. *City of Saskatoon Archives, S-COS-2(2)*

Reading, Writing & Arithmetic

Basic education was considered essential for good citizenship. By 1905 in Alberta, 526 schools offered basic education. Saskatchewan also had countless one-room schools, and many were used until the 1950s. Similar to this one, when it opened in 1924, enrollment at the Marienthal School, near Torquay on Saskatchewan's southern border, was 27 students for grades 1 - 7. The school was only 7.3 m by 10.3 m (24 by 34 ft). Classes were scheduled during summer but not in the coldest months of winter. *Milt Moyer Collection.*

This teacher and children from Bruderheimer, Alberta were photographed in 1915. In both provinces, as late as 1948, northern communities had trouble attracting teachers and achieving basic literacy and math skills. Many students quit school in elementary grades. There had been no school to attend until they were about 11-years-old, and by 16-years-old, they or their parents believed earning an income was more important than school. *Glenbow Archives, Calgary, Canada, NA 2676-6*

Enduring Values of Informed Minds

Soon after the inauguration of the two provinces, they initiated the creation of universities. In 1906, Alberta's Premier Alexander Rutherford introduced a bill for a provincial non-denominational university. It was to be open to female and male students. The first classes were offered in 1908, and a student body of about forty undergraduates included seven women. Despite such progressive steps, the university was not without controversy. Calgarians had wanted the university and believed they deserved it since Edmonton had been named the capital city. Instead, Edmonton was selected for the university while Calgary became the site for the Normal School, charged with the education of future teachers. In 1945, the school became part of the U of A

Department of Education. But Calgary's dismay at not having autonomy and full degree-granting status continued. An extensive university site was built in 1960, and finally, in 1966, U of C had full autonomy as a university. By the 21st Century, numerous smaller cities offered university courses. As well, online courses became available so students could earn degrees while never leaving home.

In Saskatchewan, the first university was nicknamed "The People's University." Legislators established the University of Saskatchewan in 1907. Located in Saskatoon, its first classes were offered in 1909. Unlike many provinces, from the beginning, Saskatchewan decided to ensure its university was nonsectarian. In addition, it would be the centre for

Shown here with the University of Alberta Students' Union is Alexander Rutherford. As well as introducing the bill that created U of A, he was Chancellor of the University from 1927 to 1941. In addition, his donation of 4 000 books became the initial holdings of the university's library. *City of Edmonton Archives, EA10-2472*

the agricultural college.

The first five buildings included an administration building, residence, agricultural engineering building, and a power house. The last three were red brick buildings, but the others, and the next "generation" of buildings were of greystone, the architecture following the tradition of collegiate gothic. The stone was glacial-till left after the great glaciers had receded, but the hard stone had to be hand-cut, making labor costs high. Those expenses changed the look of the U of S, as well as other university campuses in Alberta and Saskatchewan. In later buildings, the much loved greystone at U of S was used only as a surface covering, not for load-bearing walls.

The university was also aware of student expenses and proposed an innovative solution. In 1969, the

Posing for their photo in 1913 are staff and students of Alberta Ladies College, established at Red Deer, Alberta, in 1910. Founded by Presbyterian minister Neil Keith from eastern Canada, like most post secondary institutions – especially those for women – it had strong religious ties. Shown here, the main building was completed at a cost of $65 000, and Keith's three daughters were among the first students. However, in 1916, the college board sold the land and building to the Alberta government. The program of Alberta Ladies College moved to Edmonton. At first, it operated from Assiniboia Hall on the U of A campus, but by 1918, the college program was renamed Westminster Ladies College and operated out of the former Strathcona Hotel. In 1924, the college finally folded. *Red Deer Archives, P-202-14*

U of S adopted a policy whereby students could pay or partially pay fees with up to 300 bushels of high-grade barley. Although the university expected 500 applications and was prepared to accept 200 students under the program, only 175 applied.

Founded in 1911, Regina College became associated with U of S in 1934. In 1975, the college became a full-fledged independent university. On campus is the Saskatchewan Indian Federated College, the first college in Canada to be administered by First Nations people for First Nations students.

Industries based on both

Photographed in 1917, this library was a well-used resource at the U of S. Apart from university libraries, books were not readily available in prairie communities. Yet, reading was so important to early pioneers, far-off friends and family mailed books and magazines in many languages from various homelands. Also, women's organizations and farm associations established lending libraries, many of which also operated through the mail. Similar to other early prairie cities, Calgary had a Women's Literary Club as early as 1906, but it did not have a public library. As well, bookstores were a rarity, and despite a population of about 11 000 in 1912, Calgary had only four book stores. The Carnegie Foundation came to the rescue, funding the Memorial Park Library, the city's first public library. Strathcona, the community on the opposite side of the riverbank from Edmonton, opened its first public library in 1913. Camrose, Alberta, organized its first library in 1919. There, the town provided an office, and the IODE raised money for the librarian's salary. Even in small towns, today's libraries depend heavily on being connected to the world through the Internet. *University of Saskatchewan Archives, Photo Collection, A 874*

Old & New Industries

Not Just Pocket Change

renewable and non-renewable natural resources became big business in the twin provinces. The oldest industries and businesses in Alberta and Saskatchewan were the fur trade and prospecting for minerals. The fur trade included both pelts and buffalo robes, and the prized mineral was gold. The economic process for the fur industry was a barter system, and in southern areas, whiskey was often the payment received. Despite changing fashions and fads, furs remained important as an industry for decades. Today, mineral resources continue to fuel the economy of Alberta and have become very important in Saskatchewan as well.

Royalties from oil and gas deposits have filled and refilled the coffers of Alberta, making it one of the richest provinces in the country. The billions of dollars from petroleum allowed Alberta to retire its debt in 2004. As well, the

Canada's two interior provinces were initially explored because of fur and fashion. The fur-trading companies amassed fortunes. Eventually, farmers also began raising fur-bearing animals. Although suffering a financial blow with the emergence of anti-fur activists at the end of the 20th Century, the fur industry of Alberta and Saskatchewan remained strong long after the days of early fur traders. Routinely, fur shows were held at Regina and Edmonton. Fur ranches became a source of pelts, with farmers raising mink, fox, and other fur-bearing animals such as chinchilla. By 1945-46, trapping was the source of virtually all beaver, badger, bear, ermine (weasel), marten, muskrat, rabbit and squirrel pelts. Most mink and fox were ranch raised. Alberta ranked fourth and Saskatchewan fifth in terms of the total value of pelts provided to Canada's fur industry. *Saskatchewan Archives Board S-B 6053*

At Cairns Department Store in Saskatoon, these women pursued a career in tailoring. As important as fashion was to women, early positions varied from sweat shop conditions to situations where women tailors were considered professional and successful independent business women. (circa 1907) *Saskatoon Public Library, LH 421*

money has given provincial politicians the leeway to challenge federal directives. Alberta doesn't need federal tax money – returned as transfer payments – to the same extent most provinces need the money.

Potash is the mineral that must be considered pay dirt in Saskatchewan. The mineral is used in the fertilizer industry, and deposits significant enough to be mined were discovered in 1946 near Unity, Saskatchewan. An American company opened the first potash mine in the 1950s. Esterhazy became the site of the world's largest potash mine and refinery complex. In the late 1960s production skyrocketed, and eventually, the province supplied 95 percent of the potash produced in Canada.

However, renewable resources have been important to provincial economies too, and forestry is one of the most significant.

Long before petroleum in Alberta and potash in Saskatchewan contributed to provincial economies and coffers, coal was a mineral resource important for everything from coal oil to light lanterns, fuel for stoves, and fuel for rail transportation. Mine disasters haunted the Crows Nest Pass area. In this case, men are rebuilding a mine entrance after the Frank slide. *Glenbow Archives, Calgary, Canada, NA 147-36*

In both provinces, early control over lumbering practices was controlled through the Dominion Lands Act. Forestry reserves or timber districts could be leased from the government and lumbered in accordance with federal regulations. Some administration of natural resources was turned over to the provinces in 1926 and finally, in the 1930s, complete control of natural resources – including the right to collect royalties – was granted to the provincial governments of Saskatchewan and Alberta.

The electricity produced by dams has long been an important renewable resource, but wind power is also an important large-scale option. Prior to 2004, southern Alberta topped the list with wind farm sites, and windy Alberta outproduced all provinces. Second in production was Quebec, but it produced only about 65 percent of that generated in Alberta. The next closest was Saskatchewan, which produced 13 percent of Alberta's total.

The contemporary technological industry is not a natural resource; however, the resource industries as well as service industries and people's homes have become dependent on the new industry. The high tech world began with electricity and telephones. Everyone needed them and the demand was always for more and better. Today, the industry is booming, and Calgary has become a strong centre for technology in Canada.

Many new immigrants who needed cash took jobs as lumbermen in both provinces. These men cut trees in northern Saskatchewan. By the 1960s, although spruce and pine were lumbered in huge volumes, aspen was the most significant wood to the provinces lumbering industry. In northern areas, lumbering and re-forestation have continued to be an economic mainstay in terms of income and employment. By 2004, the industry expected a record-setting year for production and prices. *Saskatchewan Archives Board, R-A 4608*

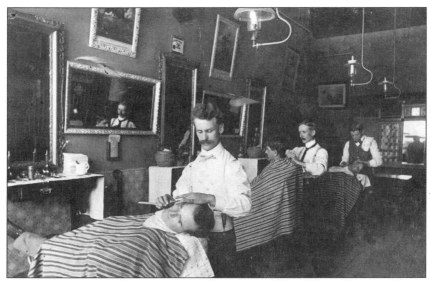

Barbershops enjoyed a brisk business early in the 1900s, and at Ott's barbershop in Lethbridge, Alberta, not a chair was empty on this day in about 1905. *Sir Alexander Galt Museum & Archives, Lethbridge, P19640394000*

The locally-owned general store or small grocery was fairly common until about the 1960s when chain stores increasingly appeared even in small towns. Corner stores, for buyers who needed only a few items, remained individually owned, but most groceries were purchased at the supermarkets. Traditionally, stores closed one afternoon a week plus Sundays, but they might be open until 9:00 p.m. once a week. Today, many supermarkets are open every day from morning until about 10:00 p.m. *Provincial Archives of Alberta, Kensit Studio, KS 57*

Black Gold and Natural Gas

Petroleum was discovered in both Saskatchewan and Alberta, but the job of finding and extracting oil and gas was more difficult in Saskatchewan, which has more sedimentation and glacial drift as an overlay for the deposits.

In May 1909, gas, with an estimated flow of one million cubic feet per day, was discovered in East Calgary. The find was lauded as the solution to power problems in Western Canada. The *Calgary Herald* editorial claimed the discovery could make Calgary the greatest manufacturing centre east of the Great Lakes.

Thirty years later, the growth of the oil industry was also evident in places such as Lloydminster, on the border between the provinces. Proving a good place to drill for crude, production in the area went from 331 barrels in 1940 to 5 000 000 barrels in 1954.

Building pipelines became an important associated industry. By 1951, an oil pipeline linked Alberta to Regina and from there to Eastern Canada. Although Saskatchewan saw revenues from petroleum, Alberta was to become the centre for the Canadian oil industry, and the province reaped billions in oil and gas-related revenues.

City of Edmonton Archive, EA 10-2959

Natural gas reserves were discovered in Saskatchewan at places such as Maple Creek, shown here in 1908. In the Medicine Hat, Alberta area, the "Old Glory" well, drilled in 1909 and owned by the CPR, had a capacity of 4 500 000 cubic feet per day. Flaring the wells was fairly common and became a tourist attraction. The city of Calgary supplied natural gas services in 1912, but natural gas was not available for consumer use in Regina until 1957. *Glenbow Archives, Calgary, Canada, NA 1368-14*

Although men were the primary employees in the petroleum industry, increasingly, paperwork created jobs traditionally held by women. This group is the stenographer pool for the CPR Department of Natural Resources at Calgary in 1915. After the 1970, increasingly women were hired for other jobs, including as landsmen and geologists. With the end of the century, more and more were entering management in the oil industry. *Glenbow Archives, Calgary, Canada, NA 5055-1*

Lurking Dangers

The photo of this Saskatchewan refinery clearly shows the general appearance of many of petroleum facilities. *Saskatchewan Archives Board, Melville-Ness Photo, S-MN-B 1395*

The first prairie refinery was built at Regina in 1916, and by 1962, the Imperial Oil refinery was massive. Edmonton's first refinery was constructed in 1948, and later, many more were built throughout the province.

One of the largest, begun in 1964, was the Great Canadian Oil Sands project at Fort McMurray. A 428 kilometre pipeline was built to carry the oil to Edmonton.

In the 1970s Syncrude built an even larger refinery, the Athabasca Tar Sand plant, which had a capacity for handling twice as much oil sands as the Fort McMurray plant. When the Athabasca project floundered financially, the federal, Alberta, and Ontario governments bailed the private enterprise out by coming up with funding for 30% of the project. Once again, Edmonton became its refinery, storage, and distribution centre.

Unfortunately, there was a downside to the heavy industry. According to the Commission for Environmental Cooperation, an agency of the North American Free Trade Agreement (NAFTA) in Canada, pollution from industrial plants in and around Edmonton was second only to that in the Durham region near Toronto.

The petroleum industry has given work to thousands, but there has been a cost. A single example of that is the plant site at Turner Valley.

Built in 1913, it was the first petroleum production site in western Canada and the oldest sour gas processing facility. After decommissioning in 1985, it became a historic site, owned by the Alberta government. Recent studies have confirmed the site is heavily polluted. Like many other petroleum-related sites, the Turner Valley facility was built near a river: in this case the Sheep River.

Today, it is common knowledge that seepage of contaminants into rivers, groundwater, and water systems is problematic.

In 2004, as a solution to the problem, diversion of the Sheep River began. The river bed will be moved 50 metres from its present course and a containment wall built, a cost estimated at $175 000. De-contaminating the site is estimated at $1.5 million, but such a process may take a decade, during which, the price tag may rise.

New techniques for drilling, recovering and refining petroleum have been developed, but the cost of rehabilitating lands used in resource development is only now being recognized.

The danger of oil and gas related refineries and used oil recycling plants near large cities has remained a disaster waiting to happen. On August 9, 1999, on Calgary's east side, a massive explosion rocked the air.

The recycling plant for Hub Oil Company caught fire. As toxic smoke rose in the air, area residents were evacuated. Others with breathing problems were cautioned to stay inside, but fortunately, lack of wind meant smoke went straight up rather than dispersing across the entire city. The fire was so intense and the danger so great, firefighters had to let the fire run its course. By 10:00 p.m. there were only half a dozen or so tanks that had not yet exploded.

At 8:30 am, April 3, 1955, smoke loomed over Calgary, creating a frightening scene. Photographer Ian Christie captured the image for the Calgary Herald. The fire looked ominous, but 44 years later, the smoke that billowed over Calgary spelled an even greater disaster with the fire at the Hub Oil petroleum recycling plant. *Glenbow Archives, Calgary, Canada, Calgary Herald File (Fires, 1945-59)*

The damage from the fire was estimated at $6 million. Five people were injured and two died.

As follow up, the Calgary Regional Health Authority surveyed 325 households in the area. Sixty percent of the residents were in the area at the time. Of the households nearest to the accident, 60% had found oil droplets in their yards and about half had additional debris, too. The residents of those homes were twice as likely as others to experience health symptoms.

These men installed wiring for the City of Edmonton Telephones. *Telephone Historical Centre, Edmonton, Alberta*

Getting wired in the early days meant being wired for telephone and electrical service, the precursor to computers and Internet. The story of telephones in the Edmonton vicinity was similar to other prairie communities.

A year after incorporation, Edmonton granted charters to a privately owned Edmonton and District Telephone Company. By the end of 1901, it had three switchboards with a capacity of 200 phone lines. Within a year, Edmontonians used 102 of the lines and surrounding communities were granted the others through a franchise and licensing system. Use expanded, and in 1903, long distance phone calls became a reality. The Edmonton system operated 24 hours a day, every day, unlike towns with service only during regular business hours.

By 1905, with pressure for municipal ownership, the city purchased its system. At the time, the Alberta government also wanted in on phones. The provincial government purchased exchanges from Bell for communities around Edmonton.

With that, Alberta Government Telephones (AGT) began to gain control over the phone industry, including rural service. By 1908, the Saskatchewan government provided urban and long distance phone service. Rural systems were owned and operated by subscribers – a financial burden for the wide-spread users, and one which led to phone co-operatives. At the time, there were about 3 000 phones in the province or one for every ninety people.

By the 1980s, both provinces enjoyed the high tech world of computers, faxes, fibre optics, cellular phones, and digital everything. Most people still received these services via phone lines or cable networks, but by 2000, that was already becoming passe.

On the Move

Getting There is Half the Fun

In the early days, there were countless wagon trails between forts and villages. Rutted paths led to ranches and farms, but eventually, provincial governments accepted the enormous responsibilities for building better roads.

Yet it was the railways that really changed the face of Alberta and Saskatchewan. Before the turn of the century, Canadian Pacific Railways (CPR) was the major player in transportation. Trains brought thousands of settlers, their personal belongings, and the goods, tools, and equipment they needed to establish farms and homes.

The CPR built countless branch lines. They did it not simply as a service to the country but because selling the land they had received from the government in exchange for building railways was lucrative. Providing the subsequent transportation for settlers and all their goods was also lucrative.

Homestead lands were available from the government too, and populations were increasing in remote areas more quickly than the CPR could build rail lines. Other players saw opportunity and entered the industry. Early in the 20th Century, rail lines reached most large communities in the two interior provinces. In 1923, Canadian Pacific, and Canadian National (CN) railways had an iron grip on railway transportation in the west. Between them, they controlled 90% of the market. Before the end of the 20th Century, service on many of

Being on the move was more than just getting from one place to another. People looked forward to the races at early fairs. Often, during them, thousands of dollars exchanged hands, but races were also commemorated in post cards such as this one. *Saskatoon Public Library, PH 95-85*

the branch lines had ceased, and railway rights-of-way were being sold to the highest bidder. Many communities were devastated by the decision, but automobiles, trucks, and airplanes had reduced the need for railways. However, freight did remain a major railway business on the prairies.

People would go to almost any extreme to arrive at church on time. This couple drives their prize-winning team of oxen, which won honors at a fair in Battleford, Saskatchewan in 1909. *Saskatchewan Archives Board, R-A 2473*

Taken at Saskatoon in about 1907, the photo shows women drivers have been around for a very long time. *Saskatoon Public Library, LH 2993*

For Saskatoon, the City of Bridges, moving back and forth across the North Saskatchewan River was crucial to the city's residents and economy. Dislodged ice during spring break-up on the river could destroy bridges. On the CNR Bridge, later named the Idylwyld Bridge, a train derailment in 1912 caused the structure to collapse. One railway car dangled precariously from the bridge as another crashed to the ice surface killing one man. Other bridges served the city well for decades. Saskatoon's Victoria bridge opened in 1907. As well as accommodating horse-pulled and motorized vehicles, the streetcar used the bridge. *Saskatchewan Archives Board S-B-9873*

By mid-20th Century, trains were the rapid transit, and Moose Jaw was a divisional point for the CPR. Shown here in 1894, Locomotive No 80 was one of many to be serviced at the roundhouse over the decades. Some claimed that without the railways, Moose Jaw would have folded. *Moose Jaw Public Library, 68-304*

Trackside Tragedies

Railways were the life blood of many small towns, and wrecks on the rails had a long history in Canada. Just east of the Alberta-Saskatchewan border, by 1912, Hanna, Alberta, became a divisional point for the Great Northern Railway, which was later acquired by CNR. There, townspeople, doctors, nurses, and railway employees saw more than their fair share of serious railway-related emergencies, and because of its location, accidents near Hanna often involved railway employees from both provinces.

The spring of 1948 brought two devastating accidents. February delivered brutal winter weather, the worst in decades. Snow was 61 centimetres (2 ft) deep, which eliminated winter grazing for livestock and created feed shortages. Meanwhile blizzards and high winds sculpted massive snow drifts. The worst of the storms began February 26, creating two weeks of unbearable weather that closed schools, led to the death of 150 sheep, stranded travellers, and curtailed rail service. But people needed coal and supplies, and ranchers needed feed deliveries, so getting trains running and keeping them running was a high priority.

By February 28, snow drifts were 15 to 20 feet deep in some places along the track. A plow train, consisting of plow, engine, water car and caboose, left Kindersley, Saskatchewan, at 8:30 a.m. Railway employees regularly travelled back and forth across the provincial border. This time the engineer for the snow plow and the fireman were from Hanna, the others from various Saskatchewan communities. The job was to clear the tracks as far as Hanna, but the going was slow. Orders had been

A number of serious train accidents occurred in the Hanna area, and often such tragedies devastated the families in both provinces.
Hanna Museum & Archives, 358 (491)

to not bury the plow, but following such orders was difficult. To get through deep drifts, the train needed speed, and speed was difficult to achieve when drifts covered the tracks.

With the risk of burying the plow in the gigantic snow banks, section-men with shovels travelled with the train to dig out the engine if it became stuck. Again and again, it was buried in the snow. Extra section-men were added to the work gang at stops along the way. By 7:00 p.m., the plow train was in the general vicinity of Hanna, with a conductor, two brakemen, and a crew of twenty in the caboose, and another five men in the plow.

Snow storms disoriented even the most experienced prairie traveller. Men in the caboose tried looking out windows to see where they were, but the windows had iced up, and smoke and steam swirled in the freezing air. Although it was no longer snowing heavily, most of the men were unable to make out landmarks.

When the engineer gave two short blasts of the train whistle to indicate to the fireman in the caboose more coal for more speed was needed, everyone assumed drifts were huge. The conductor in the caboose sensed the train was very near the Hanna yards. He grabbed the emergency air brake. When the air pressure gauge reading suddenly dropped, he knew

someone at the head of the train had reacted before he had, but it was too late.

The impact was sudden; the noise of metal on metal, deafening. Hitting an engine sitting in the rail yard, the nose of the plow forced its way under the yard engine. Steel crumpled. Men in the caboose were thrown about but had only minor injuries.

They rushed to help those in the plow and the yard engine. The scene was horrific, the worst any had ever seen. Four men who had been in the plow were badly mangled and died on impact. The fifth was pinned in steel. The rescuers called the Hanna doctor who gave the man morphine for the searing pain during the two hour ordeal of cutting him out of the twisted steel. The doctor ordered blood from Calgary that was delivered by charter plane, but the injuries were too severe, and the man died.

The engineer of the snow plow train lived, but rescuers were too late for the engineer of the yard locomotive. Pinned in his seat, the man had been scalded by steam escaping from pipes, and he died almost instantly.

Less than two months later, on April 22, 1948, west of Hanna, two CNR freight trains collided when heavy fog led to poor visibility. Again steel became twisted junk, and cars were derailed, piling one on top of another. While not fatal, people were seriously injured.

Passable Roads

Early surveys left liberal road allowances, based on the government's assumption that the new farmers would need good roads for hauling their grain and other produce to market. In reality, apart from in towns and cities, there were generally only four families per square mile and often far fewer. In rural areas in both provinces, and especially in northern areas, good trails remained a way of life until the end of World War I. In winter, more people stayed home, and in summer, basic roads were adequate.

The survey system had all but guaranteed the west would be a land where, unless there was a lake, a huge slough, big hill or mountain, most roads were straight. Lack of much traffic meant they were often narrow, but worst of all, when the snow melted or when there was a heavy rail fall, travellers faced mud and more mud.

Then came the gasoline engine and increased settlement. The resulting increase in traffic meant people wanted more and better roads. They were a provincial responsibility, but with some federal help, the provinces adopted an aggressive road-building program in the 1920s.

With its population widespread, the Saskatchewan government took road-building seriously. Generally, it has had a higher per capita expenditure on roads than other provinces. By the 21st Century, Saskatchewan surpassed all other provinces with about 250 000

In 1937, this road crew was hard at work near Penhold, Alberta, building the Calgary-Edmonton highway. *Red Deer Archives, Sid Wardle Photo, P 186-26*

km (155 350 miles) of roads. In contrast, Alberta began sub-contracting road work, and as a result, private industry bids, priorities and procedures began having a larger impact on the province's roads.

Saskatchewan went from having 22 registered motorized vehicles in 1906 to almost 96 000 in 1926. This fine car was photographed in Saskatoon in about 1910. *Saskatoon Public Library LH 3363*

Bicycle, motorcycle, and chuckwagon races all became popular at fairs. This bicycle race was held during an early exhibition at Regina. *Saskatchewan Archives Board, R-A 17, 497*

Cars were part of prairie recreation and entertainment. During some fairs, stock car racing drew crowds, and large exhibition associations built tracks for races. Stock car racing was almost a craze in 1940s Alberta. Used as a fund-raising event for war charities, the 1942 race in Calgary attracted 25 entries and drew a crowd of 1 700 people. Photographed at the Saskatoon Exhibition, this Case car was a winner at the exhibition's first stock car race in 1917. *Courtesy of Saskatoon Public Library, PH 97-71-25*

Taking to the Air

Vast spaces, far-flung communities, and natural resources in barely accessible locations made air transportation a natural solution for transporting both people and supplies. In the early days of air travel, mercy flights for the sick were also fairly common.

Bush pilots experienced both the adventure and danger of flying in remote areas where weather and adequate fuel supplies were serious concerns. Some made flights for the RCMP or federal government, including mail runs. The two provincial governments did not consider operating airlines as their mandate, but by 1947, needs were great in Saskatchewan, so the government established its own airline. Saskair operated out of Prince Albert, serving Regina, Saskatoon, and other major centres in the province including northern communities such as La Ronge and

Uranium City. In 1955, Saskair was renamed Norcanair (North Canada Air Ltd.), and by the 1980s, ownership was transferred to Time Air of Lethbridge.

In the 1950s, Athabaska Airways Ltd., with a head office in Prince Albert, served the prairies and north, the majority of its business coming from the government and public service sector. Other Saskatchewan airlines, such as La Ronge Aviation Service, offered flights to the more northerly areas. Gateway Aviation began operations in 1952, flying out of the Edmonton Municipal Airport until 1979. Over time, large airlines acquired the smaller ones at risk when issues of finances, regulation changes, accidents, or other industry-related concerns arose.

One successful aviator businessman was Max Ward. Growing up in Edmonton in the 1920s and

At the end of World War I, this bi-plane was flown in the Hanna area by pilots Les Clyde Holbrook and Les MacLeod. It was reported to be the first plane built in Alberta. *Hanna Museum & Archives*

1930s, like many other pilots of his time, he served in the air force during World War II. After the war, he established his own airline, beginning with a small operation that served the north. He expanded into national and international charter flights, and in 1989, he sold the multimillion dollar business to Canadian Airlines.

Based in Calgary, Canadian was created by the merger of Pacific Western Airlines and Canadian Pacific Airlines. Canadian was later taken over by Air Canada, but Alberta continued to challenge eastern-based commercial airlines with the emergence of Calgary-based Westjet. Calgary is home to numerous small airlines serving the petroleum industry and the north, the most renowned being Kenn Borek Air, which gained an international reputation for its high-risk mercy flights to areas as remote as the South Pole.

The generation that witnessed the first flights has given way to a generation that takes flight for granted, wanting fewer delays, and better prices and service.

An open parachute with a man dangling from it was an impressive sight in the prairie skies. By the 20th Century, parachuting, skydiving, and ballooning would increasingly become popular recreational activities, especially in the Calgary area. *Glenbow Archives, Calgary, NC 6-5430*

An interest in flying also led to model airplane clubs. The Grand Prairie Model Flying Club decorated this flying craft as a float for the parade. *Grande Prairie Regional Archives, 2003-24-16*

Culture & Influencing Culture

Getting the Word Out

As the earliest form of mass communication across the prairies, newspapers were an important source of information, politicized discussion, and gossip. The *Regina Leader*, initially advertised as the *Regina Times* and still later named the *Regina Leader Post*, was first published March 1, 1883.

The first *Phenix* [sic], which became *The Daily Phoenix*, *The Weekly Phoenix* and eventually the *Saskatoon Star Phoenix*, was published October 17, 1902.

By the end of the Second World War, A.P. (Pat) Waldron and Harris Turner, WW I veterans, started in the newspaper business, but their first paper floundered.

The Saskatoon newspaper eventually joined forces with the movement to establish a wheat pool, and enjoying the support of farm organizations, the paper was transformed into the *Western Producer*. By 1931, the Wheat Pool owned and published the paper, and the newspaper's mandate was serving the needs of western Canadians. For decades, the *Producer* was the voice of prairie farmers. Moving beyond the newspaper market, in 1962, the *Producer* published its first book. That book was *Grazing the Old Cattle Trail* by Grant MacEwan, and the publishing imprint became *Prairie Books*. In publishing, the company also focused on western Canadian voices and history.

There were many small towns that ran presses like this one at Maple Creek, Saskatchewan, circa 1912. *Saskatchewan Archives Board, R-B 9-226*

News, Politics & Opinions

The *Edmonton Bulletin* was the first newspaper published in Alberta and survived until 1951.

Initially published in 1903, the *Edmonton Journal* voiced conservative politics, as opposed to the liberalism of *The Bulletin*. Although western papers claimed to be independent and free of politics, most Alberta papers would be known as voices for conservatism.

Another Alberta newspaper, the *Macleod Gazette*, first published in 1882, was printed weekly, and has survived. In 1883, Calgary at last had its own paper, the *Calgary Herald, Mining and Ranche Advocate and General Advertiser*. The first edition rolled off a small press set up in a tent, but a century later, the *Calgary Herald* was a multimillion dollar operation. Yet it was another newspaper that garnered a truly unique reputation.

Long after the last issue of his newspaper was published, Bob Edwards was one of Calgary's best remembered journalists. His first newspaper was the *Wetaskiwin Free Lance*. In 1897, it was the first newspaper printed in the central Alberta corridor.

Opinionated and sarcastic, Edwards had both fans and detractors. He relocated to High River in 1902 and published *The Eye Opener*. By 1904, Edwards moved the paper to Calgary, and there, his satire, sarcasm and daring knew no end.

Memorable quotes included "A little learning is a dangerous thing but a lot of ignorance is just as bad," (Aug. 20, 1921) and "What with whales at Edmonton, sharks at Calgary, lobsters at Okotoks and suckers everywhere else, Alberta bids fair to become an interesting aquarium of marine curiosities." (Sept 5, 1903)

Edmonton Bulletin newsboys . City of Wetaskiwin Archives, Carl Walin Photo, Carl W. Walin fonds, 98.37-28-154

So What About Fine Arts & Heritage?

The arts and history-related groups have never had it easy in the twin provinces. They have always enjoyed strong support in Saskatchewan while Alberta's record is more erratic. Not surprisingly, during the Depression, support was limited in both provinces. Money was needed for essentials, but in later years, the provinces diverged in degrees of support.

The problem has always been numbers. Compared to the USA, BC, and eastern Canada, Alberta and Saskatchewan have small populations. There are not as many people to buy local books, records, or artwork. Theatre, music, and artistic dance are also affected.

Individuals have had phenomenal success, such as Alberta writer W.O. Mitchell. Valuing the experiences of prairie people, he used his talents to tell their stories. Those stories touched a much larger world audience. Wallace Stegner from Eastend, Saskatchewan, was another to receive acclaim, and individual musicians, dancers, actors, and artists have achieved similar recognition.

Since 1905, governments have

Residents of Regina enjoyed the music of the Rose Theatre Orchestra in 1914, but the musicians were not the first to play orchestral music in the city. Given the formal and informal gatherings of early Mounties, the city had a long musical history. The Regina City Orchestra, established in 1908, has been the only one in western Canada to continue playing every season without having to fold for a period of time for financial or other reasons. *City of Regina Archives, CORA-RPL-B-61*

addressed culture and heritage, though responsibilities shifted among departments. In 1946, the Alberta Cultural Development Branch was established. By 1975, re-organized as Alberta Culture, it focused solely on supporting the arts. During that time, the Alberta Ballet grew from a small troupe to a large touring company. Film received strong support, and Edmonton's Fringe Festival became one of Canada's great outdoor theatre events.

In Saskatchewan, Sage Hill was receiving recognition nationwide for its writing program, and Emma Lake had developed an outstanding art program. Theatre and music programs were also strong.

However, by the late 1900s, differences were more apparent. Culture came under the purview of Alberta Community Development, a department responsible for arts, sports, parks and wildlife, people with developmental disabilities, seniors, resources, human rights, citizenship, and regional community boards. Within the department, Alberta Foundation for the Arts (AFA) continued to handled arts funding, while the Alberta Historical Resources Foundation handled history-related budgets.

Government budgets revealed just how much the twin provinces diverged on arts and history funding. For the year ending March 31, 2003, just over $21 million had been budgeted for AFA. More than half went to arts promotion, such

Although Red Deer, Alberta, had a population of only about 1 800 people in 1907, the community was large enough for the play *The Queen of Hearts* to be staged at the Purdy Opera House. *Red Deer Archives, Mg-320-2-18*

as tours and advertising. Another $5 million was budgeted for film. About $3.5 million was actually slated for artistic support and development, and the rest covered other expenses. Alberta Historical Resources Foundation had a smaller budget for museums and history: just over $6 million. Even the foundation to cover the massive area of sports, recreation, parks, and wildlife had a budget of only $17 million. In contrast the business ministry, Ministry of Economic Development, spent more than $55 million.

Saskatchewan has about one million people, Alberta about three million people, who enjoyed windfall petroleum revenues. In 2002-2003 year, Saskatchewan's Department of Culture, Youth and Recreation had $43.6 million to spend. Over $12 million went to culture. Alberta had budgeted almost double – but it had three times the population. Heritage received nearly $10 million, making the Saskatchewan heritage budget almost double that of Alberta. Yet, in both, countless individuals had worked hard to establish the arts. They have organized events and donated time and money. They brought all manner of cultural experiences to local audiences and took a glimpse of western culture to the larger world.

Early in Regina's history, plays were staged by Mounties and their families, so drama already had a solid base by the time Freddy Rowan starred as the Rajah in *Cingale*e in 1925 for a Regina Theatre Production. In 1933, the Saskatchewan Drama League was founded. About sixty people attended the meeting, including the premier. By 1939, the group was affiliated with the university. In 1945, the U of S made history. It established the first drama department at the university, and it appointed Emrys Jones as head. He was the first full-time drama professor at any university in the Commonwealth, and in 1956, he founded the Canadian Theatre Centre. Jones had taken his first degree at U of A. *City of Regina Archives, CORA-RPL-B-74*

Augustus (Gus) Kenderdine was one of many great artists from Saskatchewan, who fell in love with the country and painted the landscape around him. Early in the century, he immigrated from England, and he and his family lived in a log home near Lashburn, SK. Later, Kenderdine became an art instructor for the University of Saskatchewan. He was made director of the university's School of Fine Arts and founded its summer art school at Emma Lake, the location of this photo. Such dual involvements have been commonplace for artists who must make a living through other means while pursuing their art.. *Saskatoon Public Library LH 1225*

New Years Eve, 1959, The Hungry Six band with costumes and plastic noses added to the festivities by clowning around during their performance. Styles of music and dance varied as much as the people, but generally, the style of popular music and dance reflected what was popular in America. Much of the music within communities was aimed at relaxation and entertainment. On the larger national and international stage, Alberta and Saskatchewan had their share of winners. Famous folk singer Joni Mitchell lived in Saskatoon in her youth, and K. D. Lang from Consort, Alberta, also achieved fame. *Saskatoon Public Library, B 15041*

Radio, TV, & the Silver Screen

Movies became an important form of entertainment early in the 20th Century. Regina's first movie house was a black tent, set up in the downtown area. In Edmonton, the Princess Theatre opened March 8, 1915, but the first popcorn machine did not appear in the city until 1947 at the Empress Theatre.

Sometimes, during the early days, there was live entertainment at the movie theatres too. In Calgary, Wahnita Penley took her "Charleston Line" of dancers to the Capitol Theatre stage for matinee and evening performances. She and another dance instructor also provided dancers for the annual children's Christmas movie and stage show. Held in the Grand Theatre and sponsored by the Hudson's Bay Company, it was free for children. During the year, very often, the highlight of the week for both town and rural children was going to a Saturday afternoon matinee.

Movie-making also has a long history in the west. Already in the 1920s, Alberta was recognized as a good filming location, and *Cameron of the Royal Mounted* was shot at Fort McLeod. In about 1925, *His Destiny* was filmed at Calgary. In 1936, *The Shadow of Mount Assiniboine* included scenery from Banff

Like other theatres of its time on the prairies, the Capitol Theatre (shown above) in Moose Jaw, Saskatchewan drew hundreds of children to enjoy the magic of the big screen. *Moose Jaw Public Library, Archives, 82-151*

National Park. For the films *Covered Wagon* and *The Last Frontier*, Cree from the Hobbema reserve staged a buffalo hunt at Wainwright National Park. Other early films featured Alberta landscape, but more contemporary stars such as Clint Eastwood, Marilyn Monroe, Kevin Costner, Anthony Hopkins, and Robert Duval have starred in movies that were at least partly filmed in the province. Today, the Banff International Film Festival attracts many more movie stars and directors.

Early on, Calgary, Banff, and surrounding areas became prime movie making locations. This one, *Rose Marie*, with Nelson Eddie and Jeanette MacDonald, was shot in and around Banff. *Glenbow Archives, Calgary, Canada NA 29471*

In the Twenties, radio became the source for news, weather, and market information. It brought the world of drama and musical entertainment to people in towns but more importantly to rural areas. Even the advertising informed people about products they never would have known were available. Here, Calgary children are spell-bound by the radio, but Saskatchewan residents were discovering radio too. In 1922, CKCK out of Regina became the province's first station. Early on the day for the "official opening," a thunderstorm threatened to create static for the event, but speeches were made. "Rule Britannia" was heard over the radio waves, and listeners were informed of baseball scores and market prices. *Glenbow Archives, Calgary, Canada, NA 2903-55*

Voices, Views & Vices

So What is Good, Clean Fun?

Crime and vice kept changing from decade to decade, or at least what was defined as crime and vice kept changing. Booze and gambling were often targeted vices in communities where the rules were constantly being revised.

Temperance reformers were active in both provinces, especially the Women's Christian Temperance Union. Women such as Nellie McClung and Louise McKinney were very active in the movement, as were countless women in Saskatchewan. McKinney became president of the Alberta WCTU,

then vice-president, and later acting president of the dominion association. Before her death, she was vice-president of the world organization. During the temperance campaigns prior to provincial prohibition, she met with premiers in both Saskatchewan and Alberta on the issue.

By July 1, 1915, in Saskatchewan, limited prohibition legislation had been enacted. Bars closed in June, but government liquor stores were a local option. July 21, 1915, Alberta enacted legislation, and complete prohibition

Although the photo appears to be of a poker party with drinks in 1899 at Saskatoon's first bar, the image was used as advertising for the temperance movement. *Saskatoon Public Library, LH 2681*

came into effect July 1, 1916, making Alberta the first totally dry province. By July 1, 1917, Saskatchewan was dry too. In 1924, eight years after legislation, prohibition in Alberta ended. The province opened its first government liquor stores, and bars were licensed. That year, Saskatchewan ended prohibition as well.

In Alberta, 1928 legislation restricted women to drinking only in Ladies and Escorts sections of establishments, and the legislation remained in effect until 1967. In 1971, the drinking age in the province was dropped from 21 to 18, and in 1993, liquor stores were privatized. In Saskatchewan, the drinking age remains 19.

Alberta Provincial Police officers seized this illicit still near Cardston, Alberta, in the 1920s, but there were always more to be found and shut down. In the USA, prohibition lasted from 1920 to 1933. So, illegal liquor was smuggled from Canada into the USA. With its excellent rail transportation and proximity to Chicago, Moose Jaw had its underworld. Bootlegging, gambling, and prostitution were not being curtailed, supposedly due to corrupt police. Rumor held that Al Capone and his gang made the passages beneath the city centre, the Tunnels of Moose Jaw, part of his criminal network. *Glenbow Archives, Calgary, Canada, NA 2899-13*

More Vices

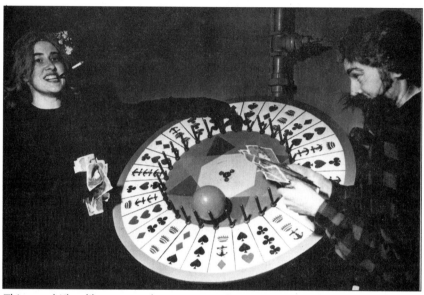

This co-ed Klondike party at the YMCA in Edmonton during 1947 did have at least one wheel, but at the time, gambling was still strictly controlled. *City of Edmonton Archives, EA 600-619B*

In the early part of the 20th Century, gambling was legislated by the Criminal Code of Canada, and amendments to the law. It was acceptable at fairs, or where profits were used for religious or charitable purposes.

By 1969, provinces could license lotteries and casinos and even operate them, but gambling was still restricted. In the 1990s, VLTs were introduced, and it seemed that the flood gates had opened. Casinos proliferated in large communities. Small communities such as Rocky Mountain House, Sylvan Lake, Barrhead,

Lacombe, and others wanted VLTs removed, but the fight was not an easy one. With reduced government funding to the nonprofit sector, charities depended on lottery funds to survive.

A similar situation was being played out in Saskatchewan. A 2003 study, *Gambling in Saskatchewan*, commissioned for the government, indicated that 86.6 percent of the respondents over 19 had gambled on everything from VLTs to card games and stocks.

Virtually the same percentage of men and women gambled.

Those with less education gambled less, and those with higher household incomes were more likely to gamble. Most people bought raffle tickets, the fewest laid bets on sports with bookies, but those who did, spent an average of $410 a month on bets. Ethnicity mattered little, but First Nations People had the most non-gamblers.

In 1913, at Whitecourt, Alberta, these young women were daring in their good times. Going into a pool hall, let alone playing billiards, was once taboo for women. Many young women even avoided walking past the pool hall since men stood outside and eyed passers-by. *Provincial Archives of Alberta, A 3228*

By the 1920s, the WCTU was warning of the dangers of cigarettes. They feared smoking would lead to greater vices, not to developing cancer. For Georgina McKay and her friends near Prince Albert, Saskatchewan, breaking rules followed by their mothers and grandmothers was a rite of passage, suggesting they were free to make choices for themselves. *Saskatchewan Archives Board R-A 1259*

Firsts for Women: Politics & Law

Saskatoon Public Library, PH 88-48

In Saskatchewan, Violet McNaughton initiated a women's section of the Grain Growers and served as the division's first president. She was also first president of the Interprovincial Council of Farm Women and president of the province's Equal Franchise Board.

By 1925, she was women's editor for the *Western Producer*. Recognizing the lack of information available for prairie women, in her columns, Violet discussed and pressured for birth control and publically funded health care. In fact, she had experience with many of the hardships felt by her women readers. Here, she drives a stone boat, and the barrel on it is labelled "Waterworks." Safe water was one of the many issues she heralded.

More Prairie Women Firsts

- Woman Magistrate/Judge in British Empire: Emily Murphy (1916, AB)
- Elected Alberta MLA: Roberta MacAdams & Louise McKinney (1917, AB)
- Elected Saskatchewan MLA: Sarah Ramsland (1919, SK)
- Provincial Cabinet Minister for Alberta: Irene Parlby, (1921, AB)
- Troop of 32 female RCMP recruits began training: (1974, SK)
- Native Woman to Practice Law in Saskatchewan: Delia Opekokew (1979, SK)
- Chief Justice of Provincial Court: Catherine Anne Fraser (1992, AB)
- Leader of the Government in the Senate: Joyce Fairbairn (1993, AB)
- Aboriginal/Metis Senator: Thelma Chalifouix (1997, AB)
- Chief Justice, Supreme Court of Canada: Beverley McLauchlin (1999, AB)

Photographed in Edmonton, Nellie McClung stands with Emmiline Pankhurst, Britain's greatest suffragette. In 1919, Pankhurst toured to help educate women about VD, a particular problem with returning soldiers. In England, Pankhurst had been imprisoned during the protests for female suffrage. While in jail, she and others had continued their protest with a hunger strike. On the Canadian prairies, Nellie had been a force in the fight for women's suffrage in both federal and provincial elections. In 1916, Saskatchewan and Alberta women won the provincial vote. In 1918, Canadian women who had the provincial franchise won the federal vote. This excluded Quebec and aboriginal women who did not have the provincial vote. Other political issues continued to be important to McClung, and she was elected to the Alberta legislature in 1921. She was also one of the Famous Five women in Canadian politics. Nellie McClung, Emily Murphy, Louise McKinney, Henrietta Muir Edwards and Irene Parlby joined forces to challenge the Constitution over whether women were persons under the law. In October of 1929, the British Privy Council answered "yes," granting Canadian women the same rights and responsibilities as men, including the right to sit in the Senate. *Honorable Justice Buzz McClung Collection*

Devastating Decade

It was a double whammy. First the stock market crashed. Then drought hit, and the 1930s became a time of lost homes and sometimes lost souls throughout Saskatchewan and Alberta. Southern Saskatchewan was hardest hit, and many would pull up stakes, move, and never return to the prairie land that had dealt them such a harsh life.

Some of those who remained went hungry. At first, there seemed no hope until many of the poor and disillusioned became angry. The social and economic circumstances created an openness to strong unions, communism, and protest parties. Conditions provided fertile ground for labor and political organizing.

As the Depression deepened, many unemployed men took to the rails, looking for work wherever they could find it. They flocked to the cities, which did not have adequate facilities and finances to properly accommodate them. Hunger strikes hit major cities in both provinces and across the country.

Unemployed men who were no longer eligible or because of residency stipulations were ineligible

Dust storms stripped fields. They filled ditches and buried fence lines creating scenes such as this one near Cereal, Alberta, in the 1930s. In southern Saskatchewan, families abandoned their farms in record numbers. They and many hard-hit Alberta grain farmers moved north, including to areas such as Peace River, Alberta, where crops were good. *Glenbow Archives, Calgary, Canada, NA 2543-45*

for city relief were simply picked up. Sent to work camps, the men were treated as criminals. Once at the camps, which were operated in a militaristic fashion, the men worked long hours at demanding physical labor – much of it related to construction and road building. They were not allowed to leave and were paid only 20 cents a day.

Both inside and outside relief and labor camps, the unrest grew, as did the men's determination to be heard by governments. "On to Ottawa," became the catch-phrase, and the unemployed, especially young men, were prepared to ride the rails to the country's capital city. By June 14, about 1 400 men reached Regina. The federal government and R.B. Bennett wanted the trek stopped at Regina. So the police moved in, forced to quell an angry crowd of rioters.

Locals did the best they could for the demonstrators, providing basic services for them at the Exhibition Grounds and raising money to cover food costs, but living conditions related to sanitation and crowding were barely tolerable. Worse yet for many was that they were still being treated like criminals. All the men wanted was to have employment and their voices heard.

This transient man rides the rails near Frank, Alberta. *Glenbow Archives, Calgary, Canada, NC 54-3604*

Organizing Labor

Although farming was certainly the primary industry, by 1912, Saskatchewan had 113 unions. The more diverse Alberta economy generated 152 unions. By 1932, the number grew to 196 in Saskatchewan and 266 in Alberta. Twenty years later, prairie totals were still far below other provinces.

Across Canada, 1919 had been crucial for unions. The Winnipeg General Strike began on May 15. The federal government ordered strikers back to work, but with rumors that the strike had been broken, on May 22, president of the Alberta Federation of Labor stated, "Any government . . . that will not recognize a representative body of organized labor has no business to exist and is heading straight for calamity." On May 26, 1 500 Calgary workers staged a sympathy strike. During the sympathy strike, railway and postal employees, as well as others, walked out. Delegates from across Canada met on June 11 for the founding convention of One Big Union.

Alberta had strong labor roots, but in later years, workers would protest repressive labor legislation. In the fall of 2004, it had the lowest minimum wage in Canada at $5.90 per hour, while Saskatchewan's minimum wage was midrange to other provinces.

In Saskatchewan, the co-operative movement went from supporting farm objectives to being a mover and shaker on the political scene. With grassroots support, the Cooperative Commonwealth Federation (CCF) was founded at a convention in Regina in 1933.

Most of the 'On to Ottawa' trekkers at Regina in 1935 were very young men. Some were spokesmen and organizers, but many were not unionized, simply wanting work and a living wage. *City of Regina Archives, CORA-RPL-B-110*

Big Bad Banks & Made-in-Alberta Credit

Social Credit, the protest party for Alberta originating in the Depression, came to power in 1935. Part of its appeal was a new approach to financial management. Premier William Aberhart and the new government saw traditional banks as making problems worse instead of better. With foreclosures, re-calling loans, and restrictive lending policies, the big banks – mostly under eastern management – were resented and severely criticized. Worse, the Depression resulted in the closure of hundreds of bank branches in small communities.

Social Credit's Made-in-Alberta answer was a moratorium on foreclosures, but the courts declared the move illegal. Another solution was the creation of its own currency, called Prosperity Certificates and nicknamed "funny money." Again, the act overstepped provincial rights since currency was a federal responsibility. Next Aberhart's government established Credit Unions.

Although banks held federal charters, in 1938, legislation created a provincial institution – the Alberta Treasury Branch. It operated through vouchers and transfer of credits from buyers to Alberta producers or manufacturers. It needed a chartered bank as backer, and the Imperial Bank of Canada became its agent. Eventually, the voucher system was phased out, and the Treasury Branches operated more like other chartered banks.

Banks such as this one at Regina in 1910 were essential for the growth of the provinces. To some, they were part of the problem during the Depression. By 1961, when the Imperial Bank and the Bank of Commerce merged to form the CIBC, the economy of the prairies was on the upswing. *City of Regina Archives, CORA B-298*

Not the Man for the Job

Richard Bedford Bennett came west to Calgary in the early 1890s. A man who could present any argument with ease, Bennett was elected to the North-West Territories' Assembly in 1898. In 1911, he won the seat for Calgary and went to Ottawa.

By 1927, he was leader of the national Conservative party and won the 1930 election. Alberta's R.B. Bennett was prime minister. His five years in office proved difficult. The stock market had crashed, the prairie was drought-stricken, and income, especially from crops in the west, plummeted. In 1919, farmers made $2.32 per bushel of wheat; by 1932, that dropped to only 35 cents a bushel.

Bennett's verbal acuity and business sense could not repair the economy. The prime minister and his party decided more structure was in order and increased government regulation, as well as control of employment and services. Bennett proposed progressive taxation, unemployment insurance, and accident and health insurance. He was prepared to revise old age pensions and promoted the idea of a minimum wage and maximum length to the work week. Also, he raised the possibility of financial support for agriculture.

North America's financial woes and the weather were cruel enemies. So in 1932, Bennett authorized relief camps for the unemployed, but they operated like prisons. The Bennett policy turned Canadians firmly against him. The camps soon earned the nickname "Bennett's Slave Camps." In addition, many Canadians had no money for basic necessities, nor "frivolities," like gasoline to fuel cars. As people began hitching their vehicles to horses, they derisively called the contraptions "Bennett Buggies."

Canadians lost faith in Bennett. In 1935, they opted for Mackenzie King to lead Canada. Feeling betrayed, Bennett left politics and moved to England. There he was made a viscount and enjoyed the honor he felt he deserved.

R.B. Bennett *Glenbow Archives, Calgary, Canada, NA 1351-3*

Dief

Enormously popular in western Canada, John Diefenbaker seemed to represent the soul of the west. His father had been a teacher in Ontario, and the heritage of his mother's family linked him to the Red River settlers. By 1903, young John and his parents moved to Fort Carlton, soon to become part of Saskatchewan, but seven years later, they were living in Saskatoon.

Learning was important in the Diefenbaker household, and John attended U of S, but with the outbreak of WW I, he enlisted and went overseas. On his return, he became a defense lawyer in small town Saskatchewan, but soon he moved to Prince Albert and got involved in politics. He was witty and enjoyed making speeches on the political stage: federal, provincial, and civic. He inspired people, but he didn't win elections, even as leader of the Saskatchewan Conservative Party. In his legal career he was increasingly successful. As a politician, he was committed, and spoke from the heart – at great length and eloquently.

Finally, in 1940, he won a seat in Parliament, but only as a back-bencher in the Opposition. It was a start, and once on the federal stage, he knew the questions to ask, and his questioning was merciless.

In 1957, as leader of the Con-

Diefenbaker was an avid hunter and fisherman. He bagged these birds in 1955. *The Diefenbaker Centre, Saskatoon, Photographs and Sides, JDG 394*

servatives, he became "Dief, the Chief," Prime Minister of Canada.

He remembered the west. Under his leadership, Canada began selling wheat to China. His government was responsible for the franchise being extended to First Nations. As well, he appointed a Blood Indian, James Gladstone of Alberta, as senator.

Through the ups and downs, most westerners loved him because he had personality and charisma. He might seem to puff and bluster, but he was their man, with the wit to prove it.

Politicians: Protests & Promises

Here, Douglas helps celebrate the 50th anniversary of the province of Saskatchewan in 1955. He continued to be a much-honored guest speaker at events. *Saskatchewan Archives Board, S-MN-B 1788*

T.C. Douglas was an important figure on both the federal and provincial political scenes. Born in Scotland, he moved with his family to Canada when he was fifteen, and became a printer's apprentice. His career goals changed and he went into the ministry. Entering college, he embraced a movement called the social gospel.

His ministry was about helping the poor and working class. When he moved to Weyburn, SK, in 1930, he discovered the suffering caused by the Depression. What he saw led him into politics, and in 1931, he attended the founding convention of the Canadian Cooperative Federation (CCF).

Four years later, he ran as their candidate in the federal election. He had dedication, charisma, and a sense of humor. As well, he stood up for the disadvantaged and for civil liberties. In 1944, after two terms in federal government, he returned to Saskatchewan where he carried the provincial CCF/NDP to power and became premier of the first socialist government in Canada.

Douglas moved back to the federal scene in 1961, where he became leader of the federal NDP. He lost his Saskatchewan seat, but won elsewhere in a bi-election, and remained leader of the federal party until 1971.

Joe Who?

Born in High River, Alberta, Joe Clark was Prime Minister of Canada from May until December, 1979. A graduate from U of A, he worked for the Progressive Conservatives but did not receive support from his home province. Nor was he well known when he won the leadership of his party. As a "progressive" conservative, he may have been too much of a "Red Tory." However, his leadership was appreciated when the Conservatives lost almost all support in the country, and the party needed a leader they could trust.

Clark meets voters at his riding in 1980. *Provincial Archives of Alberta, J5007-2*

The Manning Legacy

Ernest Manning was born in Carnduff, Saskatchewan, and moved with his family to Alberta. He attended Aberhart's Prophetic Bible Institute in Calgary. As Aberhart's prodigy, Ernest was drawn into the Social Credit movement.

In 1943, Manning succeeded Aberhart as premier, and his party remained in power until 1968.

Made an honorary chief Ernest Manning (far left) is shown here with First Nations representatives and Alberta's Lieutenant Governor J.J. Bowlen. *Glenbow Archives, Calgary, Canada, NA 2864-2398a[per]*

Years later, Ernest's son Preston Manning helped found the Reform Party. As leader, he won a seat in parliament in 1993, and four years later, he led the official opposition. In 2000, realizing the party needed a broader base of support, Preston endorsed the transformation of Reform into the Canadian Alliance party, but he lost the leadership. By 2001, Preston left federal politics.

Prairie at War

Call to Arms

As devastating and difficult as they were globally, wars were one of many ways that people of Alberta and Saskatchewan participated in the larger world. The problems that led to the wars seemed far away, but the people of the prairies, whatever their heritage, were part of Canada, and Canada was part of the global community.

Ties to Britain and, in later years, commitments to such world organizations as the United Nations (UN) meant that when military help was needed, people of the two provinces were prepared to serve. The first of the wars they served in was the Boer War at the end of the 19th Century. Men from the west, including a number of Mounties, joined up and sailed for Africa.

The west had also been strong supporters when Canada made the decision to send armed forces to WW I and WW II. By the Second World War, participation on the home front in western Canada was extensive. Enlisted men and women received some of their

From the Peace River Country, Harry Tuffill, and Alf Shattock had their photo taken with Alf's sister, Maud, before leaving for the First World War. Overseas, Alf was killed. When Harry returned, he and Maud were married. They continued to live in northern Alberta. *Grande Prairie Regional Archives, 056-01-085-4*

army training at nearby bases in major cities where other facilities were temporarily converted for the purpose.

Two other very significant programs on the prairies brought both international military and enemy soldiers to the west. The first consisted of providing bases, training personnel, and services for the Commonwealth Air Training Program. The second program was establishing Prisoner of War (POW) camps on the prairies.

By the 1990s, for economic reasons, Canada's Department of Defense decided some military bases must be closed and sold. However, in Alberta, the Edmonton and Cold Lake bases remained in use. In Saskatchewan, 15 Wing Moose Jaw was the only remaining military base, but much of the west has supported a stronger military in Canada.

For some, '9-11' (September 11, 2001) in New York seemed like a call to arms. Perhaps more than in other parts of Canada, Albertans had felt their place was beside Americans – even if it meant war. Both Alberta and Saskatchewan had huge numbers of American settlers early in the 19th Century, which made a pro-American sentiment logical. As well, by 2004, between 7 and 8 percent of Calgarians held dual citizenship or were voting Americans, the largest expatriate American community outside the continental United States.

By the end of 1914, Saskatchewan provided the British army with 1 500 horses worth $300 000, and the following year, 20 000 Saskatchewan men had enlisted. In Alberta, military training was also available in the larger communities. Soldiers, military carriages and equipment are shown here on Regina streets circa 1916. *University of Regina Archives & Special Collections 75-4, Charles Torville Papers, Photo 62, file 302, Personal Photographs - General*

These Saskatchewan troops served in the infantry. *Saskatchewan Archives Board, R-B 9328-1*

During both WW I and WW II, many women's organizations had war-related fund raisers and projects. Members of The Mothers Club in Millet, Alberta, volunteered time and sewed items for the Red Cross. Countless other women also knit socks and scarves to be sent to soldiers overseas.*Millet Archives, 190-01-51-02*

These men were from Moose Jaw, Saskatchewan, but many soldiers returned with injuries and disabilities. Helping veterans regain health or adapt to disabilities meant the emergence of veterans' hospitals in prairie cities. At Calgary in 1919, the Alberta Military Hospital [later re-named the Colonel Belcher Hospital] operated out of a renovated warehouse. With WW II, the federal government funded additional beds for veterans. The Burns Mansion was also used temporarily, but in 1943, a new facility with a capacity of 250 beds opened. Elsewhere, many veterans' hospitals had their services rolled into those of other hospitals or care facilities. *Moose Jaw Public Library, 81-136*

In the 1940s, army parades were not uncommon on the home front. This one is the COTC stationed at Saskatoon. Canadians believed the Great War was the war to end all wars. About 20 years later, young men and women from the prairies found themselves once again on battlefields in Europe. In the 1950s, they served in Korea. With the turn of the century, despite the closure of many bases in Western Canada, young peacekeepers from Alberta and Saskatchewan joined other Canadians in the military in far off places such as Bosnia and Afghanistan. *University of Saskatchewan Archives, MG 118, File 16, Photo Album, 1939-40. "Blitz," Oct. 42, Percy S. Shore*

Workers at the Alberta Foundry and Machine Shop in Lethbridge, AB, produced shell casings for the war effort. Operating successfully since 1911, the foundry had done a brisk business making iron and steel products including rails, basins, manhole covers, farm implements, mining equipment, fire hydrants, lamp posts, valves, and pumps. During WW I, it manufactured shells. Then, during WW II, it was completely devoted to the manufacture of war munitions, and 150 men and women worked in two 10-hour shifts. The foundry produced more than half a million shrapnel shells and anti-aircraft shells. *Medicine Hat Museum & Art Gallery, PC 40.13*

Women served at home and abroad in the Canadian Women's Army Corp (CWAC), or Women's Royal Canadian Naval Service (WRCNS). Also, on the home front, women repaired airplanes, worked in factories and air traffic control, became harvesters on farms, and took a wide variety of nontraditional as well as traditional jobs to help win the war. *Provincial Archives of Alberta, BL 529-3S*

Alberta became the location for the largest POW camps in Canada. Prisoners were sent by ship to Montreal and then came west by train. A small POW camp, which housed about 1 000 POW officers, was established at Wainwright. Another was located in Kananaskis Country, and a temporary one existed outside Calgary. Medicine Hat and Lethbridge camps housed the most prisoners. By June, 1946, the total number of POWs in the province was over 26 600. For various reasons, from murder to illness, some POWs died at the camps. While imprisoned in Canada, most POWs felt they had been treated with respect. Shown here, POWs bury a fellow prisoner, with a rifle salute by guards; the death may have been that of an officer. *Sir Alexander Galt Museum & Archives, Lethbridge, P19861122018*

Certificates such as this were sent to the families of the servicemen or women who died during the Second World War. Shown here, Martin Allemann immigrated from Switzerland in 1920, and by 1923, had bought a farm at Debolt, Alberta. After war was declared, he enlisted and served four years in the Canadian army. He saw duty in Britain, Italy, and Africa before being killed in action. *Millet Archives, V 002-02*

Commonwealth Air Training Program

The Canadian prairies had great terrain and weather for training pilots and others for the war effort, and the training bases would also be far from the danger of the front lines. The international agreement to initiate the Commonwealth Air Training program was signed in December, 1939, and soon communities across Canada were heavily involved – especially in Alberta and Saskatchewan. As well as training command centres, there were initial and elementary flying schools, service flying training schools, air observer schools, and flying instructors schools all over the prairies. Wireless training was also available in Calgary.

Allied military personnel from around the world trained in the western Canadian communities, but most pilots came from Britain, Australia, New Zealand, America, Norway, Poland, and Holland. Training bases near many of the small towns closed after the war, yet service men and women would return, marry, work, or see the country in better times.

The 15 Wing Moose Jaw base was turned over to private flight operations in 1946. Six years later, it was re-opened as a training field for the Royal Canadian Air Force. Today, at Moose Jaw, NATO's Flight Training in Canada program brings people from around the world to train as jet pilots. The base is also home for the Canadian Snowbirds, the country's most famous flight demonstration team.

In the 1940s, these "Fairey Battle" aircraft often performed maneuvers in the skies near Lethbridge as part of the training at the bombing and gunnery school. At Mossbank, SK, there was a second bombing and gunnery school. *Glenbow Archives, Calgary, Canada, PA 3458-7*

Prisoners at Home

George Takeyasu, shown here in the mid 1940s, was one of many Japanese settlers that chose to live in the Picture Butt area. *Sir Alexander Galt Museum and Archives, P19790284008-09*

Japanese settlements were established in Alberta as early as the first decade of the 19th Century. Many other Japanese arrived in southern Alberta during the Second World War when they were re-located from the west coast to the interior of BC, southern Alberta, or provinces further east. Most people had to start over with nothing, and many families were split up. Those who volunteered to work in the sugar beet industry were allowed to stay together.

The work was hard, days were long, and few of the farmers had adequate housing for workers. Many Japanese families lived in shacks, abandoned buildings, and other shelters where conditions were inadequate, crowded, and often unsanitary.

Alberta writer Joy Kogawa tells the moving and tragic story of the difficulties Japanese immigrants endured. Her novel *Obasan*, was published in the early 1980s.

The Lighter Side of Life

Relaxation & Tourism

Time for enjoying oneself has always been part of a balanced lifestyle. Sports events, picnics and fairs were valued social gatherings. Vacations were part of the good old summertime – or in the case of the mountain wonderlands – they were part of the good old wintertime too. The natural landscape of the two provinces offered endless opportunities for enjoying the outdoors, but visitors also needed services and places to stay. For locals, most visitors – especially those from more exotic worlds than their own – were a welcome break from life at home, work, and school.

From the time the railway was built in the mountains, Banff and Lake Louise became playgrounds attracting thousands of tourists. At the turn of the century, the building of the Chateau Lake Louise brought a dramatic change from the small chalet where a few tourists found lodging. In contrast, the Banff Springs, although repeatedly renovated, seemed to look much the same from the outside decades after it had been opened in 1888. *Milt Moyer Collection*

Bessborough Hotel in Saskatoon, Saskatchewan. *Saskatoon Public Library-LH A 1351*

In Edmonton, the castle hotel was the MacDonald. In Calgary, the Palliser Hotel opened in 1914. The CPR Hotels of Saskatchewan were later on the scene. In Regina, the Radisson opened its doors in 1928.

Bessborough Hotel, another fine castle-like hotel, was built in Saskatoon between February and December of 1931. By May, workmen had finished bricking over the bottom half of the hotel, but the framing for the top half was still visible.

Such hotels provided accommodation for the well-to-do, yet for many locals, the hotels also represented how their communities had grown and prospered. They conveyed the message that the community could now offer a sophisticated culture, as well as the basics of day-to-day living, and a grand hotel also offered increased employment opportunities.

While a status symbol for a town or city's prosperity, most local people only saw the inside of the grand hotels at graduation banquets and dances. Wealthy tourists and business people enjoyed their visits in style.

Enjoying & Protecting National Treasures

Lake Louise. Laggan.

Canoeing on Lake Louise at Banff National Park has been a popular activity since the late 1800s. *Whyte Museum of the Canadian Rockies, NA 66-2393*

The natural beauty of the two provinces led to the development of numerous provincial parks and a strong tourism industry, but the Canadian government has also recognized unique and special areas in the provinces. Already in 1887, with hunters concerned about depleting bird populations, the federal government established a bird sanctuary at Lost Mountain Lake, later a part of Saskatchewan. The bird sanctuary was the first ever created in Canada. However, the first national parks were in Alberta.

Most of the mountain range was granted to British Columbia, but the area that remained in Alberta became one of the best known mountain playgrounds in the world. In 1887, Rocky Mountains Park, which later became Banff National Park, was legislated as a protected area. In 1907, Jasper Forest Park of Canada (later named Jasper National Park) was officially established.

Early in the 20th Century, as a forest reserve with no special protection, the Waterton area was subject to extensive oil and gas exploration, and for a while, Waterton town had the name Oil City. Finally, in 1911, the federal government recognized the need to protect the beauty of Waterton, and a small area within the forest reserve became Waterton Lakes National Park.

Although the political and economic maneuvering had taken some time, in 1913, Elk Island National Park was established out of Edmonton. By 1922, Wood Buffalo National Park, straddling northern Alberta and the Northwest Territories, gained its official designation. Although it is one of the largest national parks in Canada, even today, it is far beyond the reach of most tourists.

Prince Albert National Park, the largest protected area in Saskatchewan was established in 1927. Covering an area of 3 875 square km, it is 30 percent water. There, free-roaming buffalo and white pelicans find safety.

In the south, Grasslands National Park attracts visitors. It is a refuge for the only colony of black-tailed prairie dogs in Canada. In terms of the park's human history, Sitting Bull and his people took refuge there after the Battle of the Little Big Horn.

The new kid on the block, Grasslands National Park, is just north of the American border. It took until 1981 for the federal government to realize the importance and fragility of the grasslands and begin enacting legislation that would protect some of these areas for generations to come.

At times, the protection of natural areas with their flora and fauna have been supported by federal initiatives. At other times and in other places, the provinces themselves have been responsible for parks, tourism, and environmental protection. Today, with escalating environmental awareness, there has been increased pressure on governments to preserve our land, especially as the tourism industry grows, increasing pressure on the sensitive areas themselves.

Banff National Park, one of many areas preserved to protect Canada's wildlife. *Walt Holt Photo*

Fairs, Exhibitions, & Rodeos

For decades, the popular culture of the west has been vividly presented in fairs and rodeos. Putting the community on parade has been part of the fun. Fairs also provided engaging performers, midway rides for adults and children, and opportunities to witness exotic animals, people, or acts. These community gatherings have always included sports too. Most often the featured sports have been some form of racing and rodeo competitions. The rodeo competitions require top notch athletes, but somehow rodeo sports are in a league of their own, so closely associated with the fairs that the annual community gathering is never the same without them.

Parades have remained a popular form of entertainment and were held at large and small communities in the two provinces. Apart from the military parades and a few sports parades, most were held in conjunction with the fair or rodeo. These clowns travelled the streets of Edson, Alberta, for the Empire Day parade in 1925. *Glenbow Archives, Calgary, Canada NA 461-28*

Photographed at the Edmonton Exhibition in about 1912, this elephant travelled to fairs with the Johnny Jones Show. Children were thrilled with the elephant rides, but increasingly, as awareness of humane treatment of animals grew, strict laws regarding the transport and handling of exotic animals limited their presence at the annual events.

City of Edmonton Archives, EA 160-1469

Many large cities and mid-sized communities became members of the Western Canada Association of Exhibitions. As an association, they were able to offer contracts to well-known national and international midways and acts for fair days. At the 1934 Provincial Exhibition in Regina, Royal American Shows provided four giant Ferris wheels. *Courtesy of Saskatchewan Archives Board, R-E 1994 Holiday Times, Vol 19, No. 1, p 2, 1934*

Junk sports arrived with early fairs and rodeos, but those involved were generally talented athletes. Here in 1938, "Suicide" Ted Elder, from Raymond, Alberta, boxed with a kangaroo while touring North American fairs and rodeos. *Glenbow Archives, Calgary, Canada Archives, Calgary, Canada, NA 318-73*

Wrestling a steer at Calgary's Victory Stampede in 1919, Billy Gutowski from Hardisty, Alberta, competed in Alberta and Saskatchewan between 1912 and 1925. Billy, the "Bronco Kid," won the bare back event in Drumheller in 1924 and saddle bronc riding at other stampedes. *Stockmen's Memorial Foundation, SFL 40-12-013*

To many prairie people, the best of the cowboys was Pete Knight. Dominating the saddle bronc event in the 1930s, he was World champion, Canadian champion, North American champion, and he won countless awards and trophies. He competed at rodeos through out the USA but Calgary and small prairie towns still had the thrill of seeing him ride. Knight died in California when he was bucked from a horse called Duster on May 23, 1937. *California. Courtesy of the Stockmen's Memorial Foundation, 038-Vol 1*

Women did ride in early rodeos. Crowds thrilled at the performances of "big name" American cowgirls in 1912 and 1913 but the western Canadian women who competed – most often in horse races – received little or no acclaim. This rider at the stampede in Holden, Alberta, in the 1920s remains unidentified.
National Archives of Canada, PA 030616

After a flurry of competitors in the early 1900s, for decades, women's rodeo competitions played second to men's competitions. In the 1960s, once again, cowgirls became increasingly active. By the 1970s, many outstanding women competitors were on the rodeo circuits and competing in all-girl rodeos. Barrel racing was one of their most important competitions. Nanton, Alberta, cowgirl Ruth McDougall, competed from 1974 into the1990s. In 1977, she placed first at the Calgary Stampede. Her winnings were just under $250. Again in 1986, she won first place with a purse of $816. Her total winnings at the stampede that year were $1 801. The first place purse for Ladies Barrel Racing was not raised to $50 000 until 1996.
Courtesy of the Historical Committee, Calgary Exhibition and Stampede, 345-77-20

A Sporting World

A Multitude to Choose From

The wide ranging interests of sports enthusiasts in Alberta and Saskatchewan was evident from long before provincial status was achieved. First Nations were hunters and fishermen. Bow and arrow and riding competitions were important. Snow shoeing and lacrosse were only a few of the other sports interests.

Settlers brought an interest in polo, rugby, curling, tennis, swimming, skiing, trap shooting, boxing, wrestling, judo, track and field, horseshoes, and dozens of other sports. Individuals and teams have been intent on winning, whether to achieve a personal best or to win bronze, silver or gold in international competition.

Women as well as men competed, and in the 1920s, the Edmonton Grads were the best women's basketball teams in the world. In 1986, Sharon Wood became the first Canadian woman to climb Mount Everest, but for athletes in both provinces – whether competing as teams or individually – there were endless mountains to climb and hurdles to overcome.

Again and again, important international sporting events have been held in the two provinces. In

In 1908, Ancel Maynard Bezanson's catch indicated the sport fishing potential of the northern Alberta region where he lived. He hooked this Dolly Varden in the Smokey River. Bezanson had moved to the Peace River Country in 1906, and seven years later, he was the first to drive a car over the Edson Trail. *Grande Prairie Regional Archives, 1990-30-025*

In the early years, necessary services and facilities were often basic. Sports and recreation facilities were even more so. Yet, by 1911, the people of Saskatoon did recognize and try to accommodate the need for city parks and sports facilities. *City of Saskatoon Archives*

1988, the Winter Olympics were staged in Calgary. Already western Canadians had a long history of involvement in Olympic sport, and in both summer and winter Olympics there were many heroes from both provinces. Some did not win gold, but they were truly stars.

Saskatoon's Eddie Mathers made the 1924 Olympic trials but did not go to the Olympics. Yet he was more than a sportsman, deserving his nickname "Renaissance Man." He was one of the founders of the Western Development Museum and of the Saskatoon Symphony Orchestra. Nor did age end his athletic endeavors. To celebrate his 88th birthday, he swam 88 lengths in a pool.

There have been many other Saskatchewan Olympic greats, including speed skater Catriona Le May Doan, who won gold in the 2002 Winter Olympics. The same success held true for Alberta athletes, past and present. Sometimes the struggle for gold went beyond athletic performance to fighting problems in the system.

Not only cross-country skier Becky Scott, from Vermillion, Alberta, but David Peltier and Jamie Sale received their gold medals long after the initial results.

In the 2004 Summer Olympics, Calgary's Kyle Shewfelt won gold in gymnastic floor exercises, but, many felt he deserved a second gold medal.

A wide range of other national and international competitions thrilled audiences in the two provinces as well. Annually, Spruce Meadows, near Calgary, has been the site of international equestrian competitions. In 1978, the Commonwealth Games were held in Edmonton. Stanley Cup and Grey Cup competitions, sometimes staged at home and sometimes elsewhere, have thrilled audiences, whether watching in arenas or stadiums or on the screen at home or in pubs.

Today, both provinces have their own Sports Hall of Fame, and there are countless opportunities for involvement in sports. Races are run to raise money for charitable causes, but also, the Banff to Jasper Road Race draws competitors, and Saskatoon hosts an International Marathon.

Seniors Games and Para-Olympics have growing audiences and increasing numbers of competitors. Blind sports have become important. With the help of his team members, Alberta's Ross Watson became the first blind person to climb Canada's highest peak, Mount Logan.

Today, just as in the past, sports abound and so do sports enthusiasts and heroes.

As well as demonstrating their interest in women, from their sports equipment, these eight young men appear interested in sports as varied as boxing and lacrosse. Competitive lacrosse was important to the First Nations, as well as part of the early history of the two provinces. During the 1905 inaugural celebrations at Edmonton, sports included a lacrosse match. *Saskatoon Public Library, LH 3347*

Lakes, sloughs, and grain crops were abundant in both provinces, making them the perfect landscape for duck and geese. For many people, bagging birds was one of the most important sports on the prairies. This photo shows what was possible during a morning and evening shoot of Canada geese at Unity, SK, in 1926. *Glenbow Archives, Calgary, Canada, NC 37-143*

For many early settlers, hunting was a way of putting food on the table. Both men and women became proficient shots, and entered shooting competitions. During the 1950s, the Calgary Rifle Club had a women's as well as men's competition. When gun registration became the law in Canada, Albertans, seemingly more than any other group, were opposed to registration. *Provincial Archives of Alberta, B 578*

A Hero for Two Provinces

Alex Decoteau was born at the Red Pheasant Reserve, a Cree reserve, near North Battleford, and he became a hero for First Nations, police officers, Edmontonians, and all Canadians. Both Alberta and Saskatchewan take special pride in him, and he is an honored inductee in the Sports Hall of Fame for each province.

Alex's father fought with Poundmaker at the Battle of Cut Knife Hill, and his mother's family, the Wuttunees, were well educated professionals. After his father's death, Alex left the Cree reserve

Decoteau stands with some of his medals and trophies. *City of Edmonton Police Archives*

and moved to Edmonton to live with his sister's family. The year 1909 became a pivotal time for him.

Alex joined the Edmonton Police Force, and at age twenty-two, he was the first full-time Aboriginal person in a municipal police force. That same year, he ran his first important race, one at Fort Saskatchewan, where he placed second. A month later, he won another second place in the five-mile race at the Edmonton Exhibition.

He achieved star status in Lloydminster, on June 31, 1909, when in the same event, he set the western Canada record. The next year, he placed first in four events during the Alberta Provincial Championships at Lethbridge. He won the half mile, one mile, two mile and five mile races.

At a Fort Saskatchewan race, he crossed the finish line in a ten-mile race eight minutes ahead of his nearest competitor. The competition was serious in the *Calgary Herald* Christmas Day Road Race. The six-mile race had a history extending back to the early 1900s. By 1910, he had won the race twice. Generally, Calgary is more temperate than Edmonton, but winters can be extremely cold. Christmas Day, 1910, was brutally cold.

Snow made the road slippery, and the wind was biting. Running

Decoteau in the *Calgary Herald* Christmas Day Race. *City of Edmonton Police Archives*

like the wind let alone *into* the wind would be tough. But Decoteau knew what to do. When he lined up at the starting line with fifteen other competitors, unlike his fellow competitors, he was wearing a toque, wool stockings, and gloves. Along the way, three runners dropped out. As the race neared its end, Decoteau had pulled 150 – 200 yards ahead of every one else. Nevertheless, he sprinted at the finish, and the Calgary crowds cheered.

With two wins at provincial championships, Decoteau competed in two dominion championships. In 1912, by winning the 5 000 metre race, he qualified for the Olympics in Stockholm later that year. As well, Decoteau had qualified for the 10 000 metre race, becoming the only athlete from Alberta and Saskatchewan to compete at the 1912 Olympics. At Stockholm, competing in the first heat of the 5 000 metres, he was second, but he suffered from a leg cramp and did not come home as one of the medal winners.

He ran more races, but having been promoted to a sergeant, and being among Edmonton's first motorcycle police officers, he was busy with a variety of police responsibilities.

When the world fell apart with WW I, Decoteau enlisted. While overseas, he ran and won in some war-time races, but at thirty years of age, he and his unit were sent to fight in the Battle of Passchendale. On October 30, 1917, a sniper's bullet ended his life. Alex Decoteau had run the race well, but the Great War claimed his life.

Tossing the Pigskin

Football fever was a common fall to winter affliction in both provinces and the Canadian Football League (CFL) was where the big boys played.

Despite freezing weather during November playoffs, fans donned toques and winter coats, grabbed thermoses and blankets, and went out to cheer their teams. Alberta had two CFL teams: the Edmonton Eskimos and Calgary Stampeders. Instead of splitting their support, all of Saskatchewan rooted for the Saskatchewan Roughriders.

The team survived a number of name changes. From 1910 to 1924, they played as the Regina Rowing Club. From 1924-1947, they were the Regina Roughriders, but by 1948, the teams was the Saskatchewan Roughriders. Not to be confused with the Canadian team, the Ottawa Roughriders, the Saskatchewan team was sometimes referred to as the Green Riders, the Green Machine, the Roughies, or the Wheatmen.

In 1963, quarterback Ron Lancaster, known as the Little General or the Blonde Boy Gambler, made the transition from the Ottawa Rough Riders to the Saskatchewan Roughriders, and there he came into his own as a star athlete.

Lancaster brought home the Grey Cup in 1966, and twice, won

This U of S football team had just defeated Albertans in competition. *University of Saskatchewan Archives, A 6288*

the Schenley Award. When he stopped pitching the pigskin for the team, in 1978, he had taken them to five Grey Cup finals, and had racked up 170 wins in 16 seasons. He had help. There was Gluey Hughie (Hugh Campbell) and Garnet Henley. For some, Henley was the embodiment of the Saskatchewan spirit, prepared to do whatever it took to win.

Nearing the end of one -20° C game at Taylor field, Henley leaped for a touchdown pass in the end zone, grabbed the ball, and was simultaneously tackled as he descended. He rammed headfirst into a support post for the two-foot rail that guarded the field. He broke the post and was rendered unconscious but hung on to the ball.

Ironically, Lancaster went on to coach his arch rivals for the Western League, the Edmonton Eskimos. They had their legends too.

The Eskimos won their first Grey Cup in 1954, the year "Old Spaghetti Legs," Jackie Parker, became the quarterback. During the game, he ran an 84 yard touchdown. In the following two years, he continued his success, bringing home Grey Cups in 1955 and 1956.

Among the players in all three of those winning years

was the China Clipper. Born in Calgary, Normie Kwong had been traded from the Stampeders to the Eskimos. At age eighteen, he became the youngest player to win a Grey Cup, and he was the first player of Chinese descent in the Canadian Football League. Once again, in the mid-1970s to early 1980s, the Eskimos saw glory days, and over the years, the team claimed twelve Grey Cups.

For football games, such as this one at the University of Saskatchewan, the tradition of having bands and cheerleaders help fans support their teams has been a long one. *University of Saskatchewan Archive, A 4844*

Women in Sports

By the end of the 1930s and early 1940s, women's baseball and soft ball reached enormous popularity on the prairies, and some of the women went on to play for major American teams. Well-known women's ball teams in Saskatchewan included the Aces, Ramblers, Lions, and Pats – both the Saskatoon Pats and the Regina Pats. Photographed in 1940, the Regina Pats are in the dugout at Cairn's Field, the baseball park in Saskatoon. *Saskatoon Public Library, LH 6322*

Women's hockey had an early start in Saskatchewan and Alberta. Waiting to go on the ice in 1915 are the Agros, a team from the U of S, Saskatoon. *University of Saskatchewan Archives, Jean Murray Fonds, E VII.6 -1*

Women excelled in many sports, and some became house-hold names while others were little known except in their field of endeavor. As a team, the Edmonton Grads became world renowned, with countless national and international trophies and wins. Others worked within the context of a team but became famous for individual success, such as Canmore's Sharon Wood, the first Canadian woman to climb Mount Everest, a feat accomplished in 1986. Calgary woman golfer, Paddy Arnold, won six Alberta Provincial Championships and five Dominion Championships between 1938 and 1949. Nevertheless, other sports women such this golf enthusiast, remained anonymous. *Glenbow Archives, Calgary, Alberta, PD 308-128*

Ethel Catherwood was nicknamed the Saskatoon Lily, and she was one of the city's star athletes. A talented high-jumper, she moved east for competition and training. Although few Canadian women witnessed the 1928 Olympics when she competed, they thrilled to reports of the competition. Catherwood won the gold medal in the women's high jump competition at Amsterdam, Holland, in 1928, proving that she was the best in the world. *Saskatoon Public Library, LH 663*

Gordie Howe was an all-time great in hockey. Born in 1928 at Floral, SK, he was one of nine children. The family moved to Saskatoon where he played hockey on a home-made rink in the backyard. By age fifteen, he was already a talented player, destined to become a star for the Detroit Red Wings, the National Hockey League, and all of Canada. To many, a Gordie Howe hat trick was the ultimate in success. It meant a goal, an assist and a fight in one game. Breaking records, he earned the nickname "Mr. Hockey." *Saskatoon Public Library, LHR, QC 3874-10 Gordie Howe*

Number 99!

Showing the Gretzky style he became famous for, here, the Great One goes in on goal. *Provincial Archives of Alberta, J 4853-47*

The Great One! In the world of hockey, everyone knew you were referring to Wayne Gretzky.

He was not physically large, but he broke every imaginable hockey record, 61 in total during the regular and play off season. He claimed the hearts of Edmonton hockey fans but also those all over the world, and he dominated the game in the 1980s. Born in Ontario, Gretzky was captain of the Edmonton Oilers during the 1980s, when the team won five Stanley Cups.

Gordie Howe was his hero, but during his career, Gretzky broke Howe's record by more than 1 007 points, and he scored 583 goals, 93 more than Howe had achieved.

When Gretzky was traded to Los Angeles, the disappointment for Canadian fans was unfathomable, but the trade was all about Oiler finances. Years later, November 22, 2003, when Gretzky returned to Edmonton to play in the "Old Timers" event of the Heritage Classic, fans were thrilled.

Their idol was on "home" ice. Fellow teammates from the winning years were also there: Paul Coffee, Mark Messier, Jari Kurri, and Grant Fuhr. So were other Canadian greats, but it was the 1980s Oilers that Edmontonians most wanted to watch. Weather did not stop about 52 000 joyful fans from attending the outdoor game, despite a -17° C temperature and a freezing wind.

Not Just a Skate in the Park

Figure skating has long been a popular event. The Canadian Figure Skating Championships were held in Calgary in1954, the World Championships in 1972, and Olympic Figure Skating Championships in 1988. David Peltier and Jamie Sale, both of Red Deer, became the real stars for western Canadians when they were finally declared gold medal winners for the 2002 Olympics. Few skaters could perform at the international level, but many western Canadian skating stars performed in local, regional, and national ice shows. In Saskatoon, for the 957 Figure Skating Club outdoor carnival, Heather Rennie was the captive maiden in a production called *From Outer Space. Saskatoon Public Library, B 12672*

From Saskatoon, Norman Falkner grew up by a pond and became an enthusiastic skater, but from early on, he faced hardships, such as the untimely death of his father, followed by the outbreak of the Second World War. Norman enlisted. Like thousands of others, he was badly injured in battle, and ultimately, his leg was amputated. Norman returned to Canada, but didn't give up the sport he loved. He put on one skate and stood on the ice. There was no way to gain momentum. He had to be pushed. Again and again, he fell, but he never gave up. Somehow, he learned to balance on his single skate, and so began years of impressing audiences across North America with his phenomenal talent. Eventually, he moved to Ontario, but his courage in the face of adversity made him an enduring Saskatchewan hero. *Saskatoon Public Library, PH 99-71*

Beyond Boundaries

Similar attitudes exist on many issues, but the two provinces diverged on how money should be spent and the responsibility of the province to individuals.

Early communities in Alberta and Saskatchewan built hospitals, and trained and employed health professionals, but Saskatchewan takes pride in being the birthplace of healthcare.

Alberta has largely divested itself of providing full services. Instead, privatization and user fees have been recent directions.

Alberta has no sales tax, has paid off its debt, and is growing rapidly. Saskatchewan lives with provincial debt, and it does not have enormous windfall profits from petroleum. It has a sales tax.

Saskatchewan's population is small, and growth is slow. Alberta's population is mushrooming.

Both have a history of supporting protest parties. Alberta founded the Social Credit party, strongly influenced the Reform Party, and

This 1960s protest over health care was staged at the Saskatchewan legislature. Since 1947, hospital care insurance covered every eligible citizen in the province. In 1961-1962, the plan was extended to cover universal prepaid medical care (medicare). Doctors went on strike, and protesters claimed communities would lose doctors. *Saskatchewan Archives Board, Rusty MacDonald Photo, S-RM-A 1691*

and embraced the Western Canada Concept. The population is a staunchly conservative.

By 1934, the Cooperative Commonwealth Federation (CCF) later named the New Democratic Party (NDP), was the official opposition party in Saskatchewan. Today, the provincial government and federal MPs are Conservative.

Saskatchewan has the greatest degree of alienation in Canada. Seemingly, this is due to not being a "have" province. Alberta has a higher per capita income, disposable income, and net worth than Saskatchewan, but Alberta has been far more vocal in opposition to the federal government.

In both provinces, people have suffered from low grain prices, mad cow disease, and lurking West Nile virus in mosquito populations.

The motto on Saskatchewan's crest is *Multis E Gentibus Vires* or "From Many Peoples Strength." In Alberta, the crest proclaims *Fortis et Liber*, or "Strong and Free." Their coats of arms also show similarities. Atop the shield of each province are the shared symbols of a beaver and a large royal crown. Both have red and silver sheaths around those symbols. Both have images of grain on their shields. On one side of each is a golden lion symbolizing British links. On the other side of the Alberta coat of arms is a pronghorn antelope while Saskatchewan's sports a deer. As with any fraternal twins, there are differences, but the ties that bind are enduring.

While the experience of living in mountainous areas is different than the one familiar to most Alberta and Saskatchewan residents, visiting the mountains has lifted the spirits of generations of prairie people. This striking image of an Indian chief on the Norquay chairlift near Banff presented an idea of the old world, a striking landscape, and a hint of the mechanization of the modern world. The scene was part of a movie entitled "*The Silent Force*," which was filmed in and around Banff. *Whyte Museum of the Canadian Rockies, V227-4103*

Queen of Hearts

Called the "roaring game" because of the slap of brooms on the ice, curling became Saskatchewan's official sport in 2001. Clubs formed in the early 1900s and by 1909, the Regina outdoor curling rink, featuring nine sheets of ice, was the largest in the world. Saskatchewan's men's teams captured both Canadian and World Championships, yet it was a woman curler who captured the hearts of all Canadians.

Born in 1963 and growing up in Biggar, Saskatchewan, Sandra Schmirler began her life with a physical problem. She had a club foot. Not letting the early disability affect her, by age thirteen, Sandra was curling. Biggar had built its first rink in 1914. Sandra's parents and grandparents had curled, and Sandra took to the sport too. In 1981, at the end of high school, like so many others from small towns, Sandra left Biggar to attend university. Soon, she was on the U of S's women's curling team. She moved to Regina, and there, Team Schmirler took shape.

With a smile that could win anyone's heart, Sandra became captain of a team. Friend and former teammate, Jan Betker of Regina, joined as third; playing second was Joan McCusker, originally from the village of Tonkin; and Marcia Gudereit, of Moose Jaw,

was the best lead in the country.

They had the skill and will to win, but they had more than that. They sincerely cared about each other. All were talented women confident enough to call themselves the "little girls from Saskatchewan."

Soon they were among the top competitors in the game. Atina Ford joined as alternate, and her mother, Anita Ford, became coach. With win after win, the team made it to the 1993 Scott Tournament of Hearts, the Canadian women's curling championship. They won, and Sandra was "crowned" the Queen of Hearts.

The young women married and kept commitments made to both families and team. Some games were easy victories. Others demanded resolve and concentration. Together, the team won three Canadian Women's Championships, but winning meant sacrifices too.

In the fall of 1997, Sandra gave birth to a daughter. Nine weeks later, "Schmirler the Curler" and her team qualified for the 1998 Olympics at a tournament in Brandon, Manitoba. Sandra hadn't let postpartum blues or a tired body stop her from competing.

In 1998, Team Schmirler headed to the Winter Olympics held in Nagano, Japan.

Sandra Schmirler's legacy lives on not only through the road sign but in a park at Biggar, SK. The book, *Sharing the Memories: Schmirler family, team and park*, is used as a fund raiser. *Norm Boake Photo, Biggar, SK. Also courtesy Schmirler Sign Committee, Sandra Schmirler Olympic Gold Park Fund.*

Leaving small children behind was hard for them, but they did what they had to do. While the province held its collective breath, the girls from Saskatchewan swept their way to glory. On the podium, receiving their gold medals, the young women were teary. What greater accomplishment, what greater legacy than to win gold at the Olympics?

Returning a hero, Sandra was happy and glad for more time with her husband and child. In June 1999, she gave birth to a second baby girl.

While visiting family and friends in Biggar, neck and back pains that Sandra had developed, began to be more than an inconvenience. An enlarged lymph node in her lower esophagus turned out to be cancer. The aggressive cancer didn't respond to treatment. Thirty-six-year-old Sandra was facing the fight of her life.

Still, Sandra wanted to live up to her earlier commitments. She had promised to do a live interview with CBC during the Canadian junior curling championships in Moncton, NB. In early February, 2000, despite the great difficulty, she managed to make the long trip. During the interview she spoke honestly and openly.

Winning gold was a highlight in her life, and though she did want to curl again, battling cancer put everything in perspective. Family, friends and living life to the fullest were most important. At times, Schmirler joked and smiled, and she spoke eloquently about battling the worst of foes. Emotion spilled into her words. The little girl from Saskatchewan, who represented the best of the west, spoke from her heart with dignity and courage.

When death stole her away in March 2000, Canada mourned the loss of an amazing and courageous woman, their Queen of Hearts.

Ever-Changing World

In 100 years, transportation has changed, even more than revealed in this photo. In Alberta and Saskatchewan, life has changed just as dramatically. Yet, the past has formed the present and offers insights into how rapidly technology, values, and the world may change in the future. *Saskatchewan Archives Board, Melville-Ness Photo, S-MN-B 1714*

The twin provinces have welcomed many royals, but the most important of the visits were inevitably those of reigning monarchs. Taking the train across Canada in 1939, King George VI and Queen Elizabeth thrilled prairie people, and they gathered at events and along the railway tracks to catch a glimpse of the royal couple. Queen Elizabeth II and Prince Phillip visited Regina in 1973 and again in 1987. They visited Calgary in 1959 and 1973. In Edmonton for the Commonwealth Games in 1978, the Queen is shown here greeting women dressed in traditional Ukranian attire. The Queen's visit for 2005 Centenniary of both provinces is the crowning glory of 100 years of history. *City of Edmonton Archives, EA 340-736*

Sources

Statistics used within this book were gathered from many sources. Those sources of interest to academic researchers regarding budget figures, contemporary finances, resource management, and population are the web sites for the governments of Alberta, Saskatchewan, and Canada, including Statistics Canada and Environment Canada. Significant sources for statistics related to historical populations, settlement, and natural resources were *Atlas of Saskatchewan* (1969) and *Atlas of Alberta* (1969). Also, the *Canadian Encyclopedia* (1985) provides statistical information and political/government histories.

Selected Bibliography

Babcock, D.R. *Alexander Cameron Rutherford: A Gentleman of Strathcona.* Calgary, AB: University of Calgary Press & Friends of Rutherford House, 1989.

Beckstead, Anita et al. *Sharing the Memories: Schmirler family, team and park.* Biggar, SK: Sandra Schmirler Olympic Gold Park Fund, 2002.

Black, Norman. *A History of Saskatchewan and the Old North West.* Regina, SK: North West Historical Company, 1913.

Blatherwick, John. *A History of Airlines in Canada.* Toronto: The Unitrade Press, 1989.

Blue, John. *Alberta: Past and Present, Vol. I.* Chicago, Illinois: Pioneer Historical Publishing Company, 1924.

Bocking, D.H., ed. *Saskatchewan: A Pictorial History.* Saskatoon, SK: Western Producer Prairie Books, 1979.

Brennan, J. William, ed. *Regina before yesterday.* Regina, SK: Historical Committee, 75 Anniversary Management Board, City of Regina, 1978.

Brennan, J. William. *Regina: An Illustrated History.* Toronto, ON: James Lorimer & Company and Canadian Museum of Civilization, 1989.

_____. *Building the University of Saskatchewan* (pamphlet). Saskatoon, SK: University of Saskatchewan, 1973.

Byfield, Ted, ed. *Alberta in the 20th Century, Vol. 1-12.* Edmonton, AB: United Western Communications Ltd., 1994.

_____. *Canadian Encyclopedia, Vol. 1-3.* Edmonton, AB: Hurtig Publishers, 1985

_____. *Canadian Normals, Vol 2 - SI, Precipitation 1941-1970.* Downsview, Ontario: Environment Canada, 1975.

_____. *Canadian Regional Health News Release,* November 24, 1999.

Chang, Daisy et al. *Our Chosen Land: A History of Chinese Canadians.* Toronto, ON: Chinese Canadian National Council, 1984.

Charlton, Robert et al. *The 1987 Edmonton Tornado Atlas.* Edmonton, AB: University of Alberta, no date given. (See: datalib.library.ualberta.ca/tornado)

Creelman, W.A. *Curling Past and Present.* Toronto: McClelland & Steward Ltd., 1950.

Gray, James. *R.B. Bennett: The Calgary Years.* Toronto, ON: University of Toronto Press, 1991.

_____. "Documents and Newspaper Scrapbook: Breaking New Ground–Sarah Ramsland, MLA, 1919-1925." *Saskatchewan History XLIII, no 2* (Spring 1991) 52-56.

Fooks, Georgia Green. *Prairie Prisoners.* Lethbridge, AB: Lethbridge Historical Society, 2002.

_____. *EID 2003 Annual Report, Eastern Irrigation District.* Brooks, AB: Eastern Irrigation District, 2003.

_____. *Flow Beyond the Weir: The Jubilee Edition, 1944-1994.* Compiled by George Freeman. Red Deer, AB: Western Irrigation District, 1994.

Grass, Renie & Lea Nicoll Kramer. *Tapping the Bow.* Calgary: Eastern Irrigation District, 1985.

_____. "Hail the Province of Saskatchewan." *Saskatchewan History XXXIII, no. 3* (Autumn, 1980) 81-89.

Hawkes, John. *The Story of Saskatchewan and its People II.* Chicago-Regina: The S.J. Clarke Publishing Co., 1924.

_____. *Herstory: The Canadian Women's Calendar.* Sydney, BC: Gray's Publishing Ltd., 1978, 1979,1980, 1981, 1982.

_____. *Herstory: The Canadian Women's Calendar.* Regina, SK: Coteau Books, 1995, 1996.

Humphreys, David. *Joe Clark: A Portrait.* Canada: Deneau & Greenberg Publishers Ltd., 1978.

Hunter, Douglas. *Champions: The Illustrated History of Hockey's Greatest Dynasties.* Toronto: Penguin Studio Book, 1997.

Johnston, Alex and Andy den Otter. *Lethbridge: A Centennial History.* Lethbridge, AB: City of Lethbridge and Whoop-Up Country Chapter, Historical Society of Alberta, 1985.

Jones, David, L.J. Roy Wilson and Donny White. *The Weather Factory: A Pictorial History of Medicine Hat.* Saskatoon, SK: Western Producer Prairie Books, 1988.

Kuffner, Lori. "Girls of Summer." *Western People* (18 September 1997) 8-9.

Larsen, John and Maurice R. Libby. *Moose Jaw: People, Places, History.* Regina, SK: Coteau Books, 2001.

Lefko, Perry. *Sandra Schmirler: The Queen of Curling*. Toronto: Stoddart Publishing, 2000.

MacIntosh, Robert. *Boiler Makers on the Prairies*. No city given: Lodge 146 and Lodge 555, International Brotherhood of Boilermakers, Iron Ship Builders, Blacksmiths, Forgers & Helpers, 1979.

MacRae, Archibald Oswald. *History of the Province of Alberta*. No city given: Western Canada History Co., 1912.

McCourt, Edward. *Saskatchewan*. Toronto, ON: Macmillan of Canada, 1968.

MacGregor, James. *A History of Alberta*. Edmonton, AB: Hurtig Publishers, 1972.

Palmer, Howard and Donald Smith, ed. *The New Provinces: Alberta and Saskatchewan, 1905-1980*. Vancouver, BC: Tantalus Research Ltd., 1980.

Ransom, Diane. "'The Saskatoon Lily':A Biography of Ethel Catherwood." *Saskatchewan History* 41 (1988) 81-98.

Rasmussen, Linda et al. *A Harvest Yet to Reap*. Toronto: Canadian Women's Press, 1976.

Robertson, Heather. *Salt of the Earth*. Toronto, ON: James Lorimer & Company, Publishers, 1974.

Saunders, Robert. *R.B. Bennett*. Don Mills, ON: Fitzhenry & Whiteside, 1979.

Scholz, Guy. *Gold on Ice*. Regina, SK: Coteau Books, 1999.

Silversides, Brock. *Prairie Sentinel: The Story of the Canadian Grain Elevator*. Calgary, AB: Fifth House Publishers, 1997.

Wright, J.F.C. *Saskatchewan: The History of a Province*. Canada: McClelland and Stewart Ltd., 1955.

Zuehlke, Mark. *The Alberta Fact Book*. Vancouver/Toronto: Whitecap Books, 1997.

Selected Newspapers

Calgary Herald: 23 May 1916; 17 July 1987; 19 December 2003; 30 December 2003; 15 June 2004; 2 August 2004; 4 August 2004; 11 August 2004; 19 August 2004; 25 August 2004.

Fur of Canada: Winnipeg: November, 1946.

Western Producer: 7 December 1950; 20 November 1952; 23 June 1955; 18 August 1962; 8 February 1965.

Saskatoon Star: 2 June 1934.

Selected Websites

Alberta Act & Saskatchewan Act www.solon.org/constitutions/Canada

Alberta Social Credit Party www.socialcredit.com

Alberta Sports Hall of Fame www.albertasportshalloffame.com

Archives Network of Alberta www.asalive.archivesalberta.org

Canadian provincial and territorial symbols www.campusprogram.com/reference

CBC News www.cbc.ca/news

CFL www.cfl.ca

City of Calgary: History, Fire Department www.calgary.ca

Canada's Websource for News and Information www.Cnews.canoe.ca/CNEWS/ Canada

Cotter, John. "Edmonton Flood Damage in the Millions," CP 2004/07/12Beazley, Doug. "12 20,000 evacuated from West Edmonton mall," *Edmonton Sun*, 2004/07

Edmonton Oilers www.oilersheritage.com

Edukits www.edukits.ca

Environment Canada www.ec.gc.ca/press News Releases: "Tornado at Pine Lake, Alberta - A Chronology," July 15, 2000

Glenbow Museum www.glenbow.com

Globe & Mail www.globeandmail

Government of Saskatchewan, Government Relations and Aboriginal Affairs www.iaa.gov.sk.ca

Government of Alberta www.gov.ab.ca

Legislative Buildings www.assembly.ab.ca

Prairie Gold Saskatchewan Sports, Saskatoon Public Library www.publib.saskatoon.sk.ca

Quick Facts www.sasktourism.com

Saskatchewan News Index www.library.usask.ca/sni

Statistics Canada www.statcan.ca

University of Saskatchewan www.usask.ca/archives, www.usask.ca/gallery

Index